PSYCHOLOGY OF PERSONAL ACHIEVEMENT

ARVIND UPADHYAY

Achievement is often talked about in the classroom, but often only in terms of recognising who gets the highest marks. Success and achievement can look like many different things for different students. Setting clear objectives, and helping students to develop and persevere, will help them to focus better on their own progress and develop a stronger sense of wellbeing.

"Achievement, in positive psychology, is about more than getting top marks in the class. When students can see their own progress in learning and mastering a subject or skill, they will feel a sense of achievement. For this to happen, a redefinition of success and achievement is needed in order to move the emphasis away from academic achievement. In this new definition, achievement requires:"

"clearly defined objectives, goals or expectations"

"a realistic timeframe for students to complete their work

a strong understanding of the fundamentals needed to complete a goal

a 'reward', which might be as simple as acknowledgement or feedback."

Contents

1

life is not knowledge but action

THE COMMODITY OF KINGS "The great end of life is not knowledge but action." - Thomas Henry Huxley Two words describe what this book is about: PRODUCING RESULTS! To me, success is the ongoing process of striving to become more. The road to success is always under construction, and by applying the technology in this book, I was able to produce astonishing results in a very short period of time. The power to magically transform our lives into our greatest dreams lies waiting within us all. It's time to unleash that power! Power is a very emotional word for many people, and has a negative connotation for some people, but to me, ultimate power is the ability to produce the results you desire most and create value for others in the process. Real power is shared, not imposed. It's the ability to define human needs and fulfill them both your needs and the needs of the people you care about. Although we're in an information age, information is not enough to produce the results we want. Knowledge is only potential power. Action is what unites every success. For me, real "power" is the ability to act. The results we get in life is determined by how we communicate to ourselves. In the modern world, the quality of life is the quality of communication. What we picture and say to ourselves, how we move and use the muscles of our bodies and our facial expressions will determine how much of what we know we will use.We all produce two forms of communication from which the experience of our lives is fashioned. First, we conduct internal communications: those things we picture, say, and feel within ourselves. The level of success you experience internally-the happiness, joy, ecstasy, love or anything you desire-is the direct result of how you communicate to yourself. How you feel is not the result of what is happening in your life-it is your interpretation of what is happening.

NOTHING HAS ANY MEANING EXCEPT THE MEANING WE GIVE IT through our internal communication. Secondly, we experience external communications: words. tonalities, facial expressions, body postures, and physical actions to communicate with the world. Every communication we make-internal and external- is an action, a cause set in motion, and that cause produces an effect. You might think of the process of producing emotional states by managing your internal communication as being similar to a director's job. To produce the precise results (s)he wants, the director of a movie manipulates what you see and hear. Likewise, if you can learn to manipulate your internal movie, you will be able to create the external results you want in your life. You're already producing results. They just may not be the results you desire. Most of us think of our mental states and most of what goes on in our minds as things that happen outside our control. But the truth is you can control your mental activities and your behaviors to a degree you never believed possible before. If you're depressed, you created and produced the scene in the movie you call depression by the way you communicated to yourself internally with your mind and body. It takes specific actions to produce depression or ecstasy, or any emotional state. Learning to manipulate these actions will lead you to control of your emotions and your behavior. You can run your brain as skillfully as Steven Spielberg runs his set. Each chapter of this book deals with some aspect of how to run your brain. People who have attained excellence follow a consistent path to success. I call it the Ultimate Success Formula. Here are the four steps:

"1) KNOW YOUR OUTCOME-precisely define what you want 2) TAKE ACTION 3) DEVELOP SENSORY ACUITY TO RECOGNIZE THE KINDS OF RESPONSES YOU'RE GETTINGARE YOU GETTING CLOSER TO YOUR OUTCOME, OR FURTHER AWAY FROM IT? 4) DEVELOP FLEXIBILITY TO CHANGE YOUR APPROACH IF YOU'RE NOT GETTING CLOSER TO YOUR OUTCOME."

Steven Spielberg, John F. Kennedy, Martin Luther King. Jr., Ted Turner, Tina Turner, Pete Rose, and Dean Barbara Black of the Columbia University School of Law, are people that applied the Ultimate Success Formula in their lives, and who also shared what I believe are seven fundamental character traits that they have all cultivated within themselves that give them the fire to do whatever it takes to succeed.

"7 FUNDAMENTAL CHARACTER TRAITS OF SUCCESS "

"1) PASSION-gives life power, juice, and meaning. There is no greatness without a passion to be great-great parent, athlete, scientist, artist, businessperson (see Chapter XI) 2) BELIEF-passion and belief provide the fuel toward excellence (see Chapters IV, V) 3) STRATEGY-a way of organizing resources (Chapters VII, VIII) 4) CLARITY OF VALUES-the fundamental ethical, moral, and practical evaluations we make about what's most important in our lives (Chapter XVIII) 5) ENERGY-people of excellence have all have the energy to take opportunities and shape them (Chapters IX, X) 6) RAPPORT-BONDING POWER-the ability to connect with people at a deepest levels of your heart (Chapter XIII) 7) MASTERY OF COMMUNICATION-the essence of what this book is about. People who fail take the adversities of life and accept them as limitations; people who succeed have learned to turn those adversities into challenges that teach them strength. The people who shape our lives and our cultures also have the ability to communicate a vision or a quest or a joy or a mission to others. Every chapter of this book deals in some way with mastery of internal and external communication."

This book is divided into 3 parts: Part 1: How to take charge of and run your own brain and body more effectively. Part 2: Discover what you really want in your life and communicate more effectively with others. Part 3: Discover what motivates us, what we can contribute on a larger, global scale. What if there was a way to take action that greatly accelerated the learning process-what if you could learn in minutes what someone took years to perfect? - MODELING!-see Chapter II.

"CHAPTER I-KEY POINTS What we do (our results) in life is determined by how we communicate to ourselves. In the modern world. THE QUALITY OF LIFE IS THE QUALITY OF OUR COMMUNICATION. How you feel is the direct result of how you communicate to yourself - your interpretation of what is happening. NOTHING HAS ANY MEANING EXCEPT THE MEANING WE GIVE

IT. We produce two forms of communication: 1) Internal communication-how we picture, say, and feel within ourselves 2) External communication-words, tonalities, facial expressions, body postures and physical actions EVERY COMMUNICATION WE MAKE IS A CAUSE SET IN MOTION, and that cause produces an effect (result)."

CHAPTER I-KEY POINTS (CONT.) You're already producing results. But if your result is depression, there are specific ways you are communicating with yourself-e.g., things you are doing with your body, the tonality with which you talk to yourself, the way you picture your life-it takes effort to produce any result. Your job is similar to a film director's job-you need to manipulate what you see and hear (the way you communicate to yourself). COMMUNICATION IS POWER. We're in an information age, but information is not enough. ACTION IS WHAT UNITES EVERY GREAT SUCCESS. Knowledge is only potential power. POWER IS THE ABILITY TO ACT. Real power is shared, not imposed. It's the ability to define human needs and to fulfill them - both your needs and the needs of the people you care about.

"CHAPTER I -EXERCISES 1. When you are producing the result called "happiness": a) What do you picture? b) What do you say to yourself? c) What do you feel in your body? d) Do those things now, and notice how easily you can produce that result by manipulating the way you communicate to yourself. e) If you can't think of what you see, say, etc., just act as if you can-ask yourself "If I were picturing something, what would it be?" or "If I were to say something to myself, what would I be saying to myself?" etc. 2. a) Make a list of what you feel passionate about in your life? b) What beliefs do you have about what you feel passionate about? c) How do you communicate to yourself when you feel passionate - what do you picture? what do you say to yourself? what do you feel in your body when you feel passionate?"

2

DIFFERENCE THAT MAKES A DIFFERENCE

What is the difference that makes a difference? I've been obsessed by that question for my entire life. People who succeed do not have fewer problems than people who fail. It is not what happens to us that separates failures from successes. It is how we perceive what happens and what we do about what "happens" that makes the difference. Think of W. Mitchell's two terrible accidents, and contrast it with John Belushi's external success. W. Mitchell chose to consistently communicate to himself that his experience had occurred for a purpose. His internal communication formed sets of beliefs and values that continued to direct his life from a sense of advantage rather than tragedy-even after he was burned and paralyzed. John Belushi had everything externally, but internally, he'd been running on empty for years before he died of drug abuse. Long ago, I realized that success leaves clues, and that people who produce outstanding results do specific things to create those results. I believed that if I precisely duplicated the actions of others, I could reproduce the same quality of results that they had. This is called MODELING-If you precisely reproduce the specific mental and physical actions of another person, you will get the same results-if it's possible for others in the world, it's possible for you. Richard Bandler and John Grinder, co-founders of NLP (Neuro-Linguistic Programming) found that there are three forms of mental and physical actions that correspond most directly to the quality of results we produce. In order to model effectively, these fundamental ingredients must be duplicated:

"1) Belief system-"Whether you believe you can do something or you believe you can't, you're right." 2) Mental Syntax-the way people organize their thoughts. Mental syntax is like a code-ingredients and order 3) Physiology-the mind and body are totally linked. The way you use your physiology-the way you breathe and hold your body, your posture, your facial expressions, the nature and quality of your movements-actually determines what state you're in. THE STATE YOU'RE IN THEN WILL DETERMINE THE RANGE AND QUALITY OF THE BEHAVIORS YOU'RE ABLE TO PRODUCE. We're actually modeling all the time. How does a child learn to speak? We live in a culture that's consistent enough so that what works in one place will very often work in another. The world's greatest modelers are the Japanese. The One-Minute Manager by Ken Blanchard and Spencer Johnson is a model for simple and effective management of any human relationship. It was put together by modeling some of the most effective managers in the country. Think of this program as a guidebook for conscious modeling with greater precision, a chance for you to become conscious of something you've always been doing in your life. If someone is doing something outstanding, the immediate question that should pop in your mind is, "How does (s)he create that result?"

CHAPTER II-KEY POINTS

"It's a funny thing about life; if you refuse to accept anything but the best, you very often get it." -W. Somerset Maugham People who succeed do not have fewer problems than people who fail. The only people without problems are those in cemeteries. It's not what happens to us that separates failures from successes. It is how we perceive it and what we do about what "happens" that makes the difference. "Things do not change; we change." -Henry David Thoreau Success leaves clues. I believe that if I precisely duplicate the actions of others, I can reproduce the same quality of results. One of the presuppositions of NLP is that we all share the same neurology, so if anyone in the world can do anything, you can, too, if you run your nervous system in the same way- if you're willing to pay the price in time and effort. The movers and shakers of the world are often professional modelers- the Japanese, Innovation and Entrepreneurship, The One Minute Manager, In Search of Excellence, etc.

CHAPTER II-KEY POINTS (cont.) Actually, we're modeling all the time: How does a child learn to speak? Successful businesses in one city will usually produce a success in a similar kind of city before the lag time is up. Model someone's: 1) Belief System 2) Mental Syntax 3) Physiology

"CHAPTER II-MODELING EXERCISES 1. Look around you and find someone who is excellent at some aspect of his/ her life-either personally or professionally. You don't have to admire all aspects of that person's life-a person might be superior in business judgments, and not much of a marriage partner. Remember, you're looking for excellent characteristics-no one has exactly the life you'd like to live if you look closely enough. Once you've found a person with an aspect that you would like to model, begin to ask questions that relate to that person's belief system. How to duplicate mental syntax and physiology will be dealt with in Chapters VII and IX, respectively. The foundation of modeling lies in a person's belief systems. Ask him or her questions about what they believe about their success in the area that you're modeling. Let's say you admire someone's marriage, for example, and you decide you would like to find out what the husband does that seems to cause his wife to `- love and respect him so much. So you begin: "Sam, what do you BELIEVE that makes you such a good husband?" Now, Sam may say something like, "I don't know-I'm lucky, I guess." So you'll have to probe further, "Well, if you did know what you believed about marriage and your wife that makes you successful in your marriage, WHAT WOULD IT BE?" The question, "If you did know ...." allows him to go beyond his conscious awareness and bring up beliefs that he truly does have, but is not currently conscious of. You might even have to ask the same question once or twice more if he continues to say "I don't know." But with persistence and genuine curiosity, added to the compliment you're giving him about admiring his marriage, he will eventually come out with a belief like "Well, I guess every time I look at my wife I think to myself, 'What a great person she is,'" or "I don't know where I'd be without her: she supports every aspect of my life-I'd do anything for her."

CHAPTER II-MODELING EXERCISES (CONT.) REMEMBER, YOU'RE A BELIEF SYSTEM DETECTIVE. People don't become successful by chance. There are powerful beliefs that are the foundation of a person's success. Discover those

beliefs, and I'll show you how to install them in yourself later in the book. FIND AT LEAST 5 MAJOR BELIEFS THIS PERSON HAS ABOUT THE AREA YOU'RE MODELING. 2. Find another person you would like to model. Choose someone who is excellent in a different aspect-if you chose a personal context for your first candidate, choose a person whom you admire in a professional context some aspect of his/her excellence. Model their beliefs. 3. Take the beliefs that seem to really make the difference in these people's lives, write or type them out and put them in a conspicuous place in your house and car, so that you remind yourself of beliefs you would like to have. Later on, I'll take you further into installing beliefs. CONGRATULATIONS! YOU'VE TAKEN YOUR FIRST STEP TO DISCOVERING "THE DIFFERENCE THAT MAKES THE DIFFERENCE."

3

THE POWER OF STATE

The experience of being on a roll, when you could do no wrong-or the opposite-is a result of the neurophysiological state you are in. Understanding state is the key to understanding change and achieving excellence. Our behavior is the result of the state we're in. We always do the best we can with the resources available to us, but sometimes we find ourselves in unresourceful states. A state can be defined as the sum of the millions of neurological processes happening within us, in other words, the sum total of our experience at any moment in time. The problem is, most of our states happen without any conscious direction on our part. People succeed or fail in life in direct relationship to their ability to consistently put themselves in states that support them in their achievements. Almost everything people want is some possible state-love, confidence, respect-even money, which you want in order to give you states like freedom, power, love, etc. Behavior is the result of the state we're in, and our states are created by 2 main components: 1) Internal representationsa) what and how we picture in our mind, b) what we hear and what we say to ourselves in our mind 2) Physiology-posture, biochemistry, breathing, muscular tension/relaxation INTERNAL REPRESENTATION and PHYSIOLOGY work in a cybernetic loop. Anything that affects one will automatically affect the other. To control our states, we must control and consciously direct our internal representations and physiology. The key word is "re-presentation"-we experience our world through our five senses-visual, auditory, kinesthetic, olfactory, gustatory. Through the process of generalization, distortion, and deletion, the brain takes the sensory stimuli and "represents" or filters them into an INTERNAL REPRESENTATION. Thus, your internal representation, your experience of the event, isn't precisely what happened but rather a personalized internal re-presentation-it's just one interpretation as filtered through specific personal belief, attitudes, values, and metaprograms.

This filtering process explains the huge range in human perception. One person may pay more attention to what (s)he saw, another to what (s)he heard-they look at it from different angles, and have different physiologies to begin the perception process with. Since we don't know how things really are, but only how we represent them to ourselves, why not represent them in a way that empowers ourselves and others, rather than creating limitations? The key to doing this successfully is memory management. In any experience, you have many things to focus on-no matter how terrible a situation is, you can represent it in a way that empowers you. We can represent things in a way that puts us in a positive state, or we can do the opposite. If we don't consciously direct our own minds and states, our environment may produce undesirable states. We must weed our garden by deciding what we are going to focus on. Successful people are able to gain access to their most resourceful states on a consistent basis. When we go into a state, our brain then accesses possible behavioral choices. The number of choices is determined by our models of the world-what are your behavioral choices when you're in an angry state, for example? The Firewalk teaches people how to change their states and their behaviors in a way that empowers them to take action and produce new results in spite of fear. The Firewalk helps people form a new internal representation of belief and possibility.

Most people take very little conscious action to direct their states. They wake up depressed or they wake up energized. Good breaks lift them up, bad ones bring them down. Successful people are able to summon their best when they need it, when the pressure is the greatest. People who have achieved excellence are masters of tapping into the most resourceful parts of their brain, by deciding what they are going to focus on-what they are going to represent to themselves, and thus controlling the state they access on a regular basis.

"CHAPTER III-KEY POINTS People succeed or fail in life in direct relationship to their ability to consistently put themselves in states that support them in their achievements. State change is what most people are after. Learn how to effectively run your brain in order to direct your state. Behavior is the result of the state we're in, and our states are created by 2 main components: 1) Internal representations a) what and how we picture in our mind b) what we hear and what we say to ourselves in our mind 2) Physiology-posture, biochemistry, breathing, muscular tension/relaxation INTERNAL REPRESENTATION and PHYSIOLOGY work in a cybernetic loop. Anything that affects one will automatically affect the other. Through the process of

generalization, distortion, and deletion, the brain takes the sensory stimuli and "re-presents" or filters them into an INTERNAL REPRESENTATION.THE MAP IS NOT THE TERRITORY. The key to directing your internal representations successfully is memory management. We must weed our garden by deciding what we are going to focus on-like W. Mitchell did. Life is like a river. It's moving, and you can be at the mercy of the river if you don't take deliberate conscious action to steer yourself in the direction you have predetermined. The number of behavioral choices we have is determined by our models of the world. Most people take very little conscious action to direct their states. They wake up depressed or they wake up energized. Good breaks lift them up, bad ones bring them down. Successful people are able to summon their best when they need it, when the pressure is the greatest. The Firewalk teaches people to form new internal representations of possibility.

Are you a jealous person? No, you're not. YOU ARE NOT YOUR BEHAVIOR. Remember, behavior is a result of your state you're in a jealous state, and you can change that state by changing your physiology and your internal representations-what you focus on-in an instant. "

CHAPTER III-EXERCISE 1. *Think of a time when you were in a jealous state. Remember a specific time. Go back to that specific time, and ask yourself the three questions below. (If you've never been jealous, then think of a time when you were angry at someone.) Find out HOW you created this state for yourself by discovering: a) What did you picture about that person? Were you conscious of any images about what you thought that person did or didn't do? Note how much power these pictures either have or don't have in terms of your feeling the state of jealousy. (Note: the pictures may not be that important to you, or you may not be aware of them-you may have to go to step b.) b) What did you hear or say to yourself about this experience?-i.e. the other person's voice saying what, or what did you say to yourself-note both the words and the tonality of how those words were said. c) What did you feel in your body?- what sensations did you feel in your body when you were feeling the state of jealousy-like temperature, posture, breathing, muscular tension, feeling in the stomach, facial expressions, etc. Notice which of the three representation. al systems is the most powerful for you-which has the most power to put you in the state of jealousy. You should also notice now that this is just a state, and*

can be changed by focusing on something that makes you feel good. 2. Follow the same procedure as in number 1, but choose the state of love. Remember a time when you felt totally loved or loving. Remember a specific time, and go back to that time, and discover HOW you go into the state of love, and notice the difference in pictures, internal dialogue and physiology between these two states.

4

Man is what he believes

Think of the story of Pablo Casals at 90-frail and arthritic, the very thought of playing the piano totally changed his state and thus the effectiveness of his body he believed in the transcendent power of his art, his music. Beliefs deliver direct commands to your nervous system. Handled effectively, they can be the most powerful forces for creating good in your life. On the other hand, beliefs that limit your actions and thoughts can be as devastating as resourceful beliefs can be empowering. Beliefs are the compass and maps that guide us toward our goals and give us the certainty to know we'll get there. Without beliefs or the ability to tap into them, people can be totally dis-empowered; with powerful guiding beliefs, you can see what you want and be energized to get it. The more we learn about human behavior, the more we learn about the extraordinary power that beliefs have over our lives. There have been numerous studies in which a person in a hypnotic trance is touched with a piece of ice represented to him/her as a piece of hot metal. Invariably a blister will develop at the point of contact. What counted was not reality but belief-the direct, unquestioned communication to the nervous system. The brain simply does what it's told through our beliefs. Norman Cousins talks about the placebo effect, and from his own illness and studying many others, concludes, "Drugs are not always necessary. Belief in recovery always is."

Belief is nothing but a state-a feeling of certainty-that governs behavior. The birth of excellence begins with our awareness that our beliefs are a choice. You can choose beliefs that limit you, or you can choose beliefs that support you. The biggest misconception people often have of belief is that it's a static, intellectual concept, an understanding that's divorced from action and results. Nothing could be further from the truth. Belief is the doorway to excellence precisely because there's nothing divorced or static about it. Beliefs come from a variety of sources: 1) ENVIRONMENT may be the single most potent generator of belief-ghettos, on the one hand, supporting environments that help foster beliefs about being "special" on the other. 2) EVENTS, SMALL OR LARGE-like Kennedy's assassination, and personal events we'll never forget. 3) KNOWLEDGE is one of the ways to break the shackles of a limiting environment. 4) OUR PAST RESULTS-knowing you've already achieved the result you want before-just once is usually enough. 5) CREATE IN YOUR MIND THE EXPERIENCE YOU DESIRE IN THE FUTURE AS IF IT WERE HERE NOW-experiencing results "in advance." It is important to remember that the potentials we tap, the results we get, are all part of a dynamic process that begins with belief.

· POTENTIAL

· ACTION

· BELIEF / ATTITUDE

· RESULTS

If you start with a belief system that stresses what you can't do, you tap a limited amount of your potential, and you take half-hearted action, tentative actions, which will probably lead to dismal results, and then what will these results do to your beliefs about subsequent endeavors? This is a classic downward spiral: failure breeds failure. On the positive side, however, if you begin by believing with every fiber of your being that you will succeed, you'll tap lots of your potential, take massive action, and your belief in your ability to produce even better results in the future will be affirmed. In this case, success feeds on success and each success creates more belief and momentum to success on an even higher scale. Amazingly, sometimes just not having a limiting belief is enough to ensure success, or to have an experience that disproves a particular limitation-another reason we do the Firewalk. YOUR REALITY IS THE REALITY YOU CREATE THROUGH YOUR BELIEFS. CHOOSE THEM WELL

> "*CHAPTER IV-KEY POINTS Beliefs deliver direct commands to your nervous system. Beliefs are the compass and maps that guide us toward our goals and give us the certain to know we'll get there. Belief is nothing but a state-a feeling of certainty-that governs behavior. The birth of excellence begins with our awareness that our beliefs are a*

choice. Beliefs come from a variety of sources: 1) Environment 2) Events 3) Knowledge 4) Past results 5) Creating in your mind the experience you desire in the future as if it were here now-experiencing results in advance.

BELIEF-POTENTIAL-ACTION-RESULTS-upward or downward spiral that begins with your belief-your level of certainty about your success. Sometimes just not having a limiting belief is enough to ensure success. "Good timber does not grow with ease; the stronger the wind, the stronger the trees." -J. Willard Marriott YOUR REALITY IS THE REALITY YOU CREATE THROUGH YOUR BELIEFS. CHOOSE THEM WELL!"

"Let's take a look at some of your beliefs-in terms of their sources: A. Environment. What beliefs (resourceful and unresourceful) do you currently hold that were generated by your environment? Complete the following sentences: Because of my upbringing and environment, I believe that I (am, am not, can, can't, will, will not): 1) 2) 3) 4) 5)"

"B. Significant events. First, list at least five significant events in your life-public or personal events: 1) 2) 3) 4) 5) 6) 7) 8)"

"Next, complete the following statement: 1) As a result of event #1, I believe about (life, people, my abilities, who I am, etc.) Discover the beliefs you have about the other significant events in your life by answering the same question about each one. 1) As a result of event #1, I believe: 2) As a result of event #2, I believe: 3) As a result of event #3, I believe: 4) As a result of event #4, I believe: 5) As a result of event #5, I believe: 6) As a result of event #6, I believe: 7) As a result of event #7, I believe: 8) As a result of event #8, 1 believe:"

"C. Knowledge. What are the significant books you have read, or knowledge you have gained from experience? 1) 2) 3) 4) 5) What do you believe about (life, people, who you are, why you're here) as a result of gaining the knowledge you have?"

"D. Past results. List five things you have accomplished in your life and one or two things you haven't accomplished, and discover what your

beliefs are. Most people that have attended the Firewalk seminar, for example, would say, "Because I was able to do something that ought to be impossible, I now believe that anything is possible." 1) 2) 3) 4) 5)"

"E. List five things you would you like to accomplish in your life. What would you believe about yourself, life, people, etc., if you had ALREADY ACCOMPLISHED these five outcomes? 1) 2) 3) 4) 5) If you have done these exercises honestly and thoroughly, you know a great deal more about yourself than most people ever do, and should have a pretty good idea about what causes you to experience pain and pleasure in your life. If you have skipped these exercises, you might ask yourself if you aren't worth discovering what beliefs you currently have. They will provide interesting comparisons to the beliefs I will be talking about in the next chapter."

5

THE SEVEN LIES OF SUCCESS

Our beliefs are specific, consistent organizational approaches and fundamental choices about how to perceive our lives and thus how to live them. We don't know if our beliefs are true or false. What we can know, though, is if they work-if they support us. The word "lies" is used in this chapter as a constant reminder that we do not know for certain exactly how things are, and that no matter how much we believe in a concept, we should be open to other possibilities and continuous learning. I suggest you look at these seven beliefs and decide whether they're useful for you. I've found them time and time again in successful people I have modeled. And remember, modeling begins with modeling people's belief systems of excellence. BELIEF # 1: EVERYTHING HAPPENS FOR A REASON AND A PURPOSE, AND IT SERVES US. Remember the story of W. Mitchell-this was his key belief. Successful people have an uncanny ability to focus on what is possible in a situation, no matter how much negative feedback they get from their environment. They believe that EVERY ADVERSITY CONTAINS THE SEED OF AN EQUIVALENT OR GREATER BENEFIT. Do you generally expect things to work out well, or to work out poorly? Do you see the potential in a situation, or do you see the roadblocks? Many people tend to focus on the negative more than the positive. The first step toward changing that is to recognize it. BELIEFS IN LIMITS CREATES LIMITED PEOPLE.

BELIEF #2: THERE IS NO SUCH THING AS FAILURE. THERE ARE ONLY RESULTS. People always succeed in getting some sort of results. The super successes of our culture aren't people who don't fail, but simply people who know that if they try something and it doesn't give them what they want, they've had an important learning experience. You can always learn from every human experience and can thereby always succeed in anything you do. Think of Abraham Lincoln and Thomas Edison. They knew they were getting feedback, so they could make finer distinctions about politics and leadership, science and electricity. Buckminster Fuller said: "Humans have learned only through mistakes." A possibility thinker like Dr. Robert Schuller asks the question: "What would you attempt to do if you knew you could not fail?" Take the word "failure" out of your vocabulary, and replace it with "outcome." BELIEF #3: WHATEVER HAPPENS, TAKE RESPONSIBILITY. Great leaders and achievers operate from the belief that they create their world. No matter what happens-good or bad-if they didn't cause it by their physical actions, maybe they did by the level and tenor of their thoughts. Now I don't know if this is true, but it's a useful lie-an empowering belief. And if you don't believe that you're creating your world, you then believe that you're at the mercy of circumstances-things just happen to you you're an object, not a subject.

In the area of personal communication, we say that THE MEANING OF COMMUNICATION IS THE RESPONSE YOU GET. If we try to tell someone we love them, and they get upset or hostile, the fact is, our communication may have been the trigger without our knowing it. By retaining responsibility, by changing our actions, we can change our communication-the power to change the result we produce. BELIEF #4: IT'S NOT NECESSARY TO UNDERSTAND EVERYTHING TO BE ABLE TO USE EVERYTHING. Achievers tend to be time misers-they exact the essence from a situation, take out what they need, and don't dwell on the rest. They know what's essential and what's not. I'll bet that if I asked you to explain how electricity works, you would come up with something between a blank and a sketchy answer. But you're quite capable of flicking the switch and getting the result called light. BELIEF #5: PEOPLE ARE YOUR GREATEST RESOURCE. Individuals of excellence almost universally have a tremendous sense of respect and appreciation for people. They have a sense of team, a sense of common purpose and unity. Look at Japanese business and the conclusion of the book In Search of Excellence by Tom Peters and Robert Waterman: "There was hardly a more pervasive theme in excellent companies than respect for the individual." One person, no matter how brilliant, will find it difficult to match the collaborative talents of an effective team.

BELIEF #6: WORK IS PLAY. Pablo Picasso once said, "When I work, I relax; doing nothing or entertaining visitors makes me tired." Mark Twain echoed, "The secret of success is making your vocation your vacation." That's what successful people do-they enrich their work by bringing to it the same curiosity and vitality they bring to their play. **BELIEF #7: THERE'S NO ABIDING SUCCESS WITHOUT COMMITMENT.** If there's a single belief that seems almost inseparable from success, it's that there's no great success without great commitment. Anna Pavlova once said: "To follow, without halt, one aim: there's the secret of success." It's just another way of stating the Ultimate Success Formula-know your outcome, model what works, take action, develop the sensory acuity to know what you're getting, and keep refining it until you get what you want. What do Larry Bird, Pete Rose, Tom Watson, Dan Rather, Michael Jackson have in common? I like to describe what they do with W.E.I.T. What Ever It Takes (to succeed). What if your beliefs are negative, not positive? How do you change beliefs? You've already taken the first step-awareness. You know what you want. The second step is action, learning to control your internal representations and beliefs, learning how to run your brain.

"*CHAPTER FIVE-KEY POINTS Beliefs are how we turn off and turn on our brain. We don't know if our beliefs are true or false, so we remind ourselves of that by humorously calling them "lies." SEVEN BELIEFS (LIES) OF SUCCESS 1. EVERYTHING HAPPENS FOR A REASON AND A PURPOSE AND IT SERVES US. 2. THERE'S NO SUCH THING AS FAILURE. THERE ARE ONLY RESULTS. 3. WHATEVER HAPPENS, TAKE RESPONSIBILITY. 4. IT'S NOT NECESSARY TO UNDERSTAND EVERYTHING TO BE ABLE TO USE EVERYTHING. 5. PEOPLE ARE YOUR GREATEST RESOURCE. 6. WORK IS PLAY 7. THERE'S NO ABIDING SUCCESS WITHOUT COMMITMENT.*"

"*EVERY ADVERSITY CONTAINS THE SEED OF AN EQUIVALENT OR GREATER BENEFIT. Belief in limits creates limited people. You can always learn from every human experience and can thereby always succeed in anything you do. "What would you attempt to do if you knew you could not fail?" Take the word "failure" out of your vocabulary, and replace it with "outcome." THE MEANING OF COMMUNICATION IS THE RESPONSE I GET. Successful people aren't necessarily the ones with the most information, the most knowledge, but they are the most effective at using what they know. Some workaholics focus on work so much because they love it so much-they look at work the way most of us look at play ."*

CHAPTER V-EXERCISE *Compare the seven "lies" of success to your beliefs from the exercise for Chapter IV. What would happen if you installed these seven beliefs, and lived "as if" these beliefs were true? What changes do you think would happen in your life? Take some time to look at how your beliefs would be affected if you adopted the beliefs of successful people I have presented to you in this chapter. What would you no longer be able to believe about people, events, life, your abilities, etc. that used to limit you? And what kinds of successes would you be likely to have if you replaced some of your old beliefs with these new ones?*

6

MASTERING YOUR MIND: HOW TO RUN YOUR BRAIN

People don't usually lack resources: they lack control over their resources, or don't know how to get access to their resources. This chapter teaches you how to be in control of your states and, therefore, in control of your actions. I see our neurology as a jukebox that has records of our experiences that will be played back at any time if the right stimulus in our environment is triggered. So we can choose to remember experiences or push buttons that play "songs" of happiness and joy, or we can push buttons that create pain. If, however, you hold the traditional therapeutic model that we have deep-seated negative experiences that build up inside like a fluid and finally burst and overflow, and you follow a therapeutic plan of re-experiencing those negative experiences-i.e., hitting the same button that creates pain time and time again-you may be reinforcing the very negative states you want to change. So let's discover not only how to push the buttons that play the pleasure "songs," but also how to push a button that used to play a sad song, but instead now brings up an ecstatic one-or even learn to re-record over the disk and take the old memories and change them. We look at the structure of human experience, not the content. We look for answers as to "how" someone creates pain and pleasure. We don't ask "why" questions that bring up the content. The difference between how you produce the state of depression versus the state of ecstasy is the way you structure your INTERNAL REPRESENTATIONS.

"We structure our internal representations through our five senses, and primarily through the three major modalities (representational systems): visual (V), auditory (A), kinesthetic (K). You might consider your senses the ingredients from which you build any experience or result. But as any good cook will tell you, you have to know the precise quantity of each ingredient as well in order to get the specific result. We refer to the quantities of each modality as SUBMODALITIES. We can change two things about the way we represent events in our life. We can change what we represent-thus, for example. if we imagine the worst possible scenario, we can change to picturing the best possible scenario. Or we can change how we represent something-for example, some people find that picturing something as being very, very large is critical for a state of great motivation. Other people find that the specific tone of voice they use when they talk to themselves makes a major difference in their level of state of motivation. Submodalities are the smallest and most precise building blocks that make up the structure of human experience. Here's a list of virtually all of our possible submodalities: Visual: 1. Movie or still frame 2. Panorama or framed (if framed, the shape of the frame) 3. Color or black and white 4. Brightness 5. Size of picture (life size, larger or smaller) 6. Size of central object(s) 7. Self in or out of picture 8. Distance of picture from self 9. Distance of central object from self 10. 3-D quality 11. Intensity of color (or black and white) 12. Degree of contrast 13. Movement (if so, fast or slow tempo) 14. Focus (which parts-in or out) 15. Intermittent or steady focus 16. Angle viewed from 17. Number of pictures (shifts) 18. Location 19. Other?"

"Auditory: 1. Volume 2. Cadence (interruptions, groupings) 3. Rhythm (regular, irregular) 4. Inflections (words marked out, how) 5. Tempo 6. Pauses 7. Tonality 8. Timbre (quality, where resonating from) 9. Uniqueness of sound (gravelly, smooth, and so on) 10. Sound move around-spatial 11. Location 12. Other? Kinesthetic: 1. Temperature 2. Texture 3. Vibration 4. Pressure 5. Movement 6. Duration 7. Steady-intermittent 8. Intensity 9. Weight 10. Density 11. Location 12. Other? For pain: 1. Tingling 2. Hot-Cold 3. Muscle tension 4. Sharp-Dull 5. Pressure 6. Duration 7. Intermittent (such as throbbing) 8. Location 9. Other?"

you the way it has in the past. You can let it flash you any picture or sound or feeling, and you can respond automatically on cue, like a Pavlovian dog responding to a bell. Or you can choose to consciously run your brain yourself by manipulating your submodalities. If you have not fully done the exercises on the tape, DO SO NOW. This chapter will be of very little use without having done these. Manipulating submodalities gives you precise control about how you represent anything in your mind, and therefore, control over your state. Discovering your key submodalities for intensifying your resourceful states will allow you to enhance the wonderful experiences in your life, and minimize the intensity of your unresourceful states. If submodality manipulation seems like a strange thing to do, think about the way we describe experiences in life in terms of submodalities: "Something is weighing heavily on my mind," "My future looks bright (or dim)," "That person blows things out of proportion," "I have a mental block," "That person is really hot" or "Cool as a cucumber," "You have a distorted image of what happened," "She has a colorful personality," "He only sees things as black and white," "She has many dimensions to her personality," "He looks askance at everything," "His perception is askew," "He has a grave tone of voice," "My life is like a pressure cooker-ready to explode all over everything" "I'm vibrating with excitement," "That person's thinking is very dense," etc. What if you said "that really weighs lightly on my mind," or "that person just shatters what other people see as mental blocks," etc. If you have incessant internal dialogue that you don't want to hear, just turn down the volume, make it softer, farther away and weaker, or hear it nag in an incredibly sexy tone of voice, "You can't do that." Your level of motivation (like any other state) can be directed with submodalities. Use the following, chart to note what your submodalities are for motivation and lack of motivation, as you contrast the two states in the exercise on the tape.

"What if you were to take all the things you hate to do but believe you must and attach to them the submodalities of pleasure? REMEMBER, FEW THINGS HAVE ANY INHERENT FEELING. You've learned what is pleasurable and what is uncomfortable: You can simply re-label these experiences on the jukebox and immediately create new feelings about them. What if you took all your problems, shrank them down, and put a little distance between them and you? THE POSSIBILITIES ARE ENDLESS. YOU'RE IN COMMAND! These submodality changes are great, but what's going to keep them from changing back. The SWISH PATTERN makes these changes automatic-it takes internal

representations that normally produce states of unresourcefulness and causes them to automatically trigger new internal representations that put you in the states that you desire. The best part of the SWISH PATTERN is that once you implant it effectively, you don't have to think of it again-it happens automatically, without any conscious effort.

HOW TO DO A SWISH PATTERN: Step 1. Identify the behavior you want to change. Now make an internal representation of that behavior as you see it through your own eyes. If you want to stop biting your fingernails, imagine a picture of you lifting our hand, bringing your fingers to your lips, and biting your nails. Step 2. Once you have a clear picture of the behavior you want to change, you need to create a different representation, a picture of yourself as you would be if you made the desired change and what that change would mean to you. You might picture yourself taking your fingers away from your mouth, creating a little pressure on the finger you were going to bite, and seeing your nails perfectly manicured and yourself as well dressed, magnificently groomed, more in control, and more confident. The picture you make of yourself in that desired state should be disassociated. The reason for this is that we want to create an ideal internal representation, one that you will continue to be drawn to rather than one you feel you already have. Step 3. "Swish" the two pictures so that the unresourceful experience automatically triggers the resourceful experience. Once you hook up this triggering mechanism, anything that used to trigger biting your nails will now trigger you into a state where you are moving toward that ideal picture of yourself. Thus, you're creating a whole new way for your brain to deal with what in the past may have upset you. Here's how to do the swish: Start by making a big bright picture of the behavior you want to change. Then, in the bottom right-hand corner of that picture, make a small dark picture of the way you want to be. Now take that small picture, and in less than one second, have it grow in size and brightness and literally burst through the picture of the behavior you no longer desire. As you do this process, say the sound "whoosh" with all the excitement and enthusiasm you can. I realize this may sound a bit juvenile. However, saying "whoosh" in an excited way sends a series of powerful, positive signals to your brain. Once you've set up the pictures in your mind, this whole process should only take about as long as it takes to say the word "whoosh". Now in front of you is a big, bright, focused, colorful picture of how you want to be. The old picture of how you were has been smashed to smithereens. The key to this pattern is speed and repetition. You must see and feel that small dark picture become huge and bright and explode through the big picture, destroying it and replacing it with an even bigger, brighter picture of how you want things to be. Now experience the great feeling of seeing things the way you want them. Then open your eyes for a split second in order to break the state. When you close your eyes again, do the swish once more. Start by seeing the thing you want to change as large, and then have your small picture grow in size and brightness and explode through-Whoosh! Pause to experience it. Open your eyes. Close your eyes. See what you want to change. See the original picture and how you want to change it. Whoosh it again. Do this five or six times as fast as you can. Remember, the key to this is speed: and to have fun doing it. What you are telling your brain is, see this, "Whoosh!" Do this, see this, "Whoosh!" Do this, see this, "Whoosh!" Do this . . . until the old picture automatically triggers the new picture, the new states, and thus the new behavior. You can also do a SWISH PATTERN with fears and frustrations. Do the exercise on the tape. You can also do the slingshot approach-imagine a slingshot in front of you. Between the two posts is a picture of the present behavior you want to change. Place a small picture of how you want to be in the sling. Then mentally watch this little picture being pulled farther and farther back until the sling is stretched as far as possible. Then let it go. Watch as it explodes right through the old picture in front of you and into your brain. Association and disassociation are submodalities that are critical for everyone to be able to use effectively. There are many people who spend most of their time disassociated. The advantage is if you avoid very deep emotions about some things and events in your life, you will have more resources to handle them. However, if this is your consistent pattern of representing most of your experiences in life, you're really missing what I call the juice of life, a tremendous amount of passion and joy. On the other hand, if all or the vast majority of your internal representations are fully associated, you may find yourself an emotional misfit - on an emotional roller coaster. The key to life is balance, including the perceptual filters of association and disassociation-we need to associate and disassociate consciously.

We can use submodalities for changing beliefs. Remember, a belief is nothing but a feeling (state) of certainty about something. How do you represent that state of certainty? The way you represent any other state - through specific submodalities. Do you think you'd be as certain about something that is dim, unfocused, tiny, and far away in your mind as you would be about something that is just the opposite? Do the same exercise you did with the state of motivation to change feelings of certainty. Start with a belief you're totally sure of, then think of something you wish you were sure of (you might pick one of the seven "lies" of success from the last chapter). Run through the submodalities and make the contrastive analysis, notice the differences between the submodalities of the two beliefs, then reprogram the submodalities of the belief you're not sure of so they match the belief you are sure of. YOU'RE IN CHARGE! You can do the same thing with physical pain. You can greatly reduce or remove physical pain by disassociating yourself by seeing (as opposing to feeling) the pain outside yourself, and seeing its shape and size, moving it ten feet away, make it bigger and smaller, causing it to grow and explode through the ceiling and then shrink it down. Push the pain into the sun and watch it melt to nothing and then come down to earth as sunshine to feed the plants. And if you doubt your ability to do this, haven't you done this unconsciously many times you got caught up in something else, or something exciting happened, and you forgot about the pain .YOU CAN CHANGE ANYTHING YOU FEEL IN YOUR LIFE BY CHANGING THE WAY YOU REPRESENT IT IN YOUR MIND, AND SUBMODALITIES GIVE YOU TOTAL CONTROL OF HOW YOU REPRESENT ANYTHING! TAKE THAT CONTROL BACK AND MAKE YOUR LIFE A MASTERPIECE! You might notice that this chapter has plenty of exercises in submodalities on the tape, so I won't add any new ones here. If you commit yourself to decreasing the intensity in the way you represent the areas of your life that cause you pain by changing your submodalities, and increasing the intensity of the way you represent resourceful areas of your life, you will reap unimaginable rewards. If, in addition, you increase your level of motivation in areas that are important to you, remove fears, change beliefs, and learn to control physical pain, you will become powerful in every area of your life. And if you learn to change behaviors by using the SWISH PATTERN, you will not even recognize yourself.

REMEMBER, THE ONLY TWO THINGS YOU'LL EVER WANT TO CHANGE ARE: 1) HOW YOU FEEL 2) HOW YOU BEHAVE. Submodalities and the SWISH PATTERN give you total control over both of these areas. What if you believed with absolute certainty and commitment that now that you know of these powers, as a king or queen, you MUST wield this sovereign power?! I wonder what your kingdom would look like, and feel like?"

KEY POINTS

People don't usually lack resources; they lack control over their resources, or don't know how to get access to their resources. I see our neurology like a jukebox that has records of our experiences that will be played back at any time if the right stimulus in our environment is triggered. So we can choose to remember experiences or push buttons that play "songs" of happiness and joy, or we can push buttons that create pain. We look at the structure of human experience, not the content. We look for answers as to "how" someone creates pain and pleasure. We don't ask "why" questions that bring up the content. We structure our internal representations through our five senses, and primarily through the three major modalities (representational systems): visual (V), auditory (A). kinesthetic (K). You might consider your senses the ingredients from which you build any experience or result. We refer to the quantities of each modality as SUBMODALITIES. We can change two things about the way we represent events in our life. We can change what we represent-or we can change how we represent something. Submodalities are the smallest and most precise building blocks that make up the structure of human experience.We can use submodalities for changing beliefs. Remember, a belief is nothing but a feeling (state) of certainty about something. How you represent that state of certainty? The way you represent any other state-through specific submodalities. YOU CAN CHANGE ANYTHING YOU FEEL IN YOUR LIFE BY CHANGING THE WAY YOU REPRESENT IT IN YOUR MIND, AND SUBMODALITIES GIVE YOU TOTAL CONTROL OF HOW YOU REPRESENT ANYTHING! TAKE THAT CONTROL BACK AND MAKE YOUR LIFE A MASTERPIECE! REMEMBER, THE ONLY TWO THINGS YOU'LL EVER WANT TO CHANGE ARE: 1) HOW YOU FEEL 2) HOW YOU BEHAVE. Submodalities and the SWISH PATTERN give you total control over both of these areas.

"*We can use submodalities for changing beliefs. Remember, a belief is nothing but a feeling (state) of certainty about something. How you represent that state of certainty? The way you represent any other state-through specific submodalities. YOU CAN CHANGE ANYTHING YOU FEEL IN YOUR LIFE BY CHANGING THE WAY YOU REPRESENT IT IN YOUR MIND, AND SUBMODALITIES GIVE YOU TOTAL CONTROL OF HOW YOU REPRESENT ANYTHING! TAKE THAT CONTROL BACK AND MAKE YOUR LIFE A MASTERPIECE! REMEMBER, THE ONLY TWO THINGS YOU'LL EVER WANT TO CHANGE ARE: 1) HOW YOU FEEL 2) HOW YOU BEHAVE. Submodalities and the SWISH PATTERN give you total control over both of these areas.*"

"*EXERCISE Most of Chapter Six is a series of submodality exercises, so your exercise for this chapter is to go back through this tape, and DO THESE EXERCISES NOW if you haven't done them. Stop the tape often if it goes too fast, but discipline yourself to take control of running your brain by taking control of your submodalities.*"

7

THE SYNTAX OF SUCCESS

The meaning of an experience is determined by the order of the signals provided to the brain. We'll use the word STRATEGY to describe the combinations of all the factors that create any result: kinds of internal representations, the necessary submodalities, and the required syntax. We have a strategy for producing just about anything in life: the feeling of love, attraction, motivation, decision, depression, whatever. If we discover what our strategy for love is, for example, we can trigger that state at will. A nice metaphor for the components and use of strategies is that of baking. If someone makes the greatest chocolate cake in the world, can you produce the same quality results? Of course you can, if you have that person's recipe. A recipe is nothing but a strategy, a specific plan of what resources to use and how and when to use them to produce a specific result. Now the baker may have worked through years of trial and error before finally developing the ultimate recipe. You can save years by following the baker's recipe, by modeling what the baker did. In the "baking" of human experience, the ingredients are our five senses and the amounts of the ingredients are the submodalities. In a recipe, though, you also need to know in what order to add the ingredients-that's the strategy. The building blocks of syntax are two different levels of sensory input: internal and external. For example, what you see in the outside world is visual-external (Ve). When you picture something in your mind-a favorite beach scene, for example-it is a visual-internal (Vi) experience. A train whistle you hear is auditory-external (Ae), a voice you hear in your head is auditory-internal-digital (Aid)-the sound itself of your voice would be auditory-internal-tonal (Ait). You can feel the texture of the armrest of the chair, or the heat of the sun on your body kinesthetic-external Me), or you can have a deep feeling of emotion inside that makes you feel good or bad-kinesthetic-internal (Ki). If you wanted to model an expert skier, for example, but couldn't actually meet him/her to ask the appropriate questions, you could watch the skier to see what his/her technique is (Ve), and then you might move your body in the same motions.

(Ke), until they feel like part of you (Ki). Next you would want to make an internal picture of an expert skier (Vi). Then you would make a new visual internal image, this time a disassociated image of yourself skiing (Vi). Next you would step inside that picture and, in an associated way, experience how it would feel to perform the same action precisely the way the expert skier did (Ki). One crucial area where understanding strategies and syntax can make a major difference is teaching and learning. Why can't some kids learn? I'm convinced there are two major reasons. First, we often don't know the most effective strategy for teaching someone a specific task. Second, teachers seldom have an accurate idea of how different kids learn. Even so-called "learning-disabled" kids are often "strategy-disabled." One teacher I worked with found that 90% of her "disabled" kids had auditory or kinesthetic spelling strategies. Let me explain why those are poor strategies for getting the result of spelling well. If you're not spelling effectively, the problem is the way you're representing words to yourself. So what's the best strategy for spelling? It's certainly not kinesthetic. It's difficult to feel a word. It's not really auditory, because there are too many words you can't sound out effectively. Spelling entails the ability to store visual external characters in a specific syntax that can be easily accessed at any time. Another aspect of learning is chunking. Generally, people can consciously process only five to nine chunks of information at once. People who learn rapidly can master even the most complex tasks because they chunk information into small steps and then reassemble them into the original whole. If you wanted to spell a word like "Albuquerque," you need to break it down into three smaller chunks like this: Albu/quer/que. Your exercise for this chapter is to use the spelling exercise on the tape to practice seeing the letters in your mind (Vi), then reassembling them on paper. Do this with a few words each day, and very soon your brain will be conditioned to access words visually. Any word you'll probably ever need to learn to spell is already in the files in your brain, so like with all the other resources, all you need to do is practice getting access. TEACH YOURSELF TO BE A GREAT SPELLER or install any other strategy by modeling the syntax as well as the submodalities of someone's internal representations.

"KEY POINTS *The meaning of an experience is determined by the order of the signals provided to the brain. We'll use the word STRATEGY to describe the combinations of all the factors that create any result: kinds of internal representations, the necessary submodalities, and the required syntax. We have a strategy for producing just about anything in life: the feeling of love, attraction, motivation, decision, depression, whatever. A nice metaphor for the components and use of strategies is that of baking. If someone makes the greatest chocolate cake in the world, can you produce the same quality results? Of course you can, if you have that person's recipe. A recipe is nothing but a strategy, a specific plan of what resources to use and how and when to use them to produce a specific result. Even so-called "learning-disabled" kids are often "strategy-disabled." People who learn rapidly can master even the most complex tasks because they chunk information into small steps and then reassemble them into the original whole.*"

"EXERCISE *If you are not an excellent speller, take three additional words and learn to spell them using the strategy described on this tape. (If you haven't learned to spell "Albuquerque" in the exercise on the tape, learn it before you do the next part of this exercise.) Make sure you chunk longer words into smaller chunks-3 or 4 letters each, put the word up and to your left, and learn each chunk at a time. Remember, do not say the letters either out loud or to yourself-just get the visual picture of the letters inside your head. If you have any difficulty "seeing" the letters inside your head, close your eyes suddenly, and you'll be able to see the lingering image. Practice maintaining that image while you memorize the picture of those letters, chunk by chunk. When you've learned the chunks, spell the words backwards. Note that there is no way to spell something backwards without having used the appropriate visual internal strategy.*"

8

HOW TO ELICIT SOMEONE'S STRATEGY

The key to eliciting strategies is knowing that people will tell you everything you need to know about their strategies. They'll tell you in words. They'll tell you in the way they use their body. They'll even tell you in the way they use their eyes. You can learn to read a person as skillfully as you can learn to read a map or a book. People tend to use a particular part of their neurology visual, auditory, or kinesthetic-more than others. Just as some people are right-handed and others are left-handed, people tend to favor one mode over the others. People who are primarily visual tend to see the world in pictures, and they tend to speak quickly, because they're trying to keep up with the pictures in their brain. Their heads are up, they breathe high in their chest, and they talk about how things "LOOK" to them, how they "IMAGINE" and "PICTURE" things. People who are more auditory tend to be more selective about the words they use. They have more resonant voices, and their speech is slower, more rhythmic, and since words mean a lot to them, they are careful about what they say. They tend to say things like "That SOUNDS right to me" or "I can HEAR what you're SAYING." Their heads are either balanced or slightly cocked (as in listening), they breathe evenly, from the diaphragm or the whole chest. People who are more kinesthetic tend to be even slower. They react primarily to feelings. Their voices tend to be deep, and their words often ooze out like molasses. They breathe low in the stomach, their heads are usually down, the neck muscles are relaxed, and they talk about "GRASPING" for something "CONCRETE." Things are "HEAVY," and they need to "GET IN TOUCH" with their "FEELINGS."

"You can also see what representational system – a person is using by watching their eyes. The chart below shows what eye positions are related to which representational system, and a few questions you can ask to get a person to access those representational systems. A longer list of questions is on the tape. EYE ACCESSING CUES VR Visual Remembered: Seeing images of things seen before, in the way they were seen before. Sample questions that usually elicit this kind of processing include: "What color are your mother's eyes?" "What does your coat look like?" VC Visual Constructed: Seeing images of things never seen before, or seeing things differently than they were seen before. Questions that usually elicit this type of processing include: "What would an orange hippopotamus with purple spots look like?" "What would you look like from the other side of the room?" AC Auditory Constructed: Hearing internal auditory sounds not heard before, or hearing them differently than they were heard before. Questions that may elicit this type of processing include: "If you were to make up a song right now, what would the first few bars sound like?" "If your mother and I were to sing the National Anthem together, what would that sound like?" AR Auditory Remembered: Remembering sounds heard before. Questions that usually elicit this kind of processing include: "What's the last thing I said?" "What does your alarm clock sound like?" AD Auditory Digital: Talking to oneself. Statements that tend to elicit this kind of processing include: "Say something to yourself that you often say to yourself." "Recite the Pledge of Allegiance." K Kinesthetic: Feeling emotions, tactile sensations (sense of touch), or proprioceptive feelings (feelings of muscle movement). Questions that elicit this kind of processing include: "What does it feel like to be happy?" "What is the feeling of touching a pine cone?" "What does it feel like to run?"

"All you need to do is get people to experience their strategy and take careful note of what they do specifically to get back into it. The key to effective elicitation of a person's strategy is putting the person in a fully "associated" state. State is the hotline to strategy. It's the switch that opens the circuits to a person's unconscious. So you must put the person back into the kitchen (like the baker)-back to the time when (s)he was experiencing the particular state-and then find out what was the very

first thing that caused him/her to go into that state. Was it something (s)he SAW (Ve) or HEARD (Ve)? Or was it the TOUCH of something or someone? After the person tells you what happened first, watch that person and ask, "What was the very next thing that caused you to be in that state? Was it...?" and so on, until that person has reconstructed his/her strategy. EVERY STRATEGY ELICITATION FOLLOWS THIS PATTERN. STRATEGY ELICITATION Can you remember a time when you were totally X'd? Can you remember a specific time? Go back to that time and experience it ... (get them in state) As you remember that time ... (keep them in state) A. What was the very first thing that caused you to be X'd? Was it something you saw? Was it something you heard? Was it the touch of something or someone? What was the very first thing that caused you to be totally X'd?"

After you (saw, heard, or were touched), what was the very next thing that caused you to be totally X'd? B. Did you . . . make a picture in your mind? say something to yourself? have a certain feeling or emotion? What was the very next thing that caused you to be X'd? After you did A and B (saw something, said something to yourself, and so on), what was the very next thing that caused you to be totally X'd? C. Did you . . . make a picture in your mind? say something to yourself? have a certain feeling or emotion? or did something else happen? What was the very next thing that caused you to be X'd? Ask if the person was very X'd at this point (attracted, motivated, whatever). If yes, elicitation is complete. If no, continue eliciting syntax until congruent completion of state. The next step is simply to elicit the specific submodalities of each representation in this person's strategy. So if the first step of the strategy was visual, you would ask: What about what you saw (visual external)? Then you would ask: What was it specifically about what you saw that motivated you? Was it the size of it? Brightness of it? The way it moved?

"Continue this process until you have all the submodalities for the strategy. Then simply talk about something you want to motivate that person to do by using the same syntax and the same key submodality words and then judge by the results you produce in that person's state. Understanding strategy is absolutely essential to success in sales. You might begin, "I noticed you're using our competitor's copy machine. I'm curious. What was the very first thing that caused you to want

to buy that machine? Was it something you saw or read about it ...or did someone tell you about it? Or was it the way you felt about the salesperson or product itself?" These questions may seem a little strange, but a salesperson who has established rapport will say, "I'm curious because I really want to fill your needs." You can also figure out what your own love strategy is. Love strategies are different from many other strategies in one key way. Instead of a three- or fourstep procedure, there's usually only one step. There's one touch, one thing to say, or one way of looking at a person that makes him or her feel totally loved. Does that mean everyone needs just one thing to feel loved? No. I like to have all three, and I'm sure you do too. I want someone to touch me in the right way and tell me they love me and show me they love me. But just as one sense often dominates overall, one way of expressing love instantly unlocks your combination, making you feel totally loved. How do you elicit someone's love strategy? You should already know ...but here it is in a written form:"

ELICITING LOVE STRATEGIES Can you remember a time when you felt totally loved? Can you remember a specific time? As you go back to that time and experience it . . . (get the person in state): V. In order for you to feel these deep feelings of love, is it absolutely necessary for your partner to show you (s)he loves you by . . . taking you places? buying you things? looking at you in a certain way? Is it absolutely necessary that your partner show you that (s)he loves you in this way for you to feel totally loved? (Judge by physiology.) A. In order for you to feel these deep feelings of love, is it absolutely necessary for your partner to . . . tell you (s)he loves you in a certain way? (Judge by physiology.) K. In order for you to feel these deep feelings of love, is it absolutely necessary for your partner to . . . touch you in a certain way? (Judge by physiology.) Now elicit the submodality. How specifically? Show me, tell me, demonstrate for me. Test inside and outside the strategy. Judge by congruent physiology.

A minority of people will at first come up with two love strategies instead of just one. They'll think of a touch, and they'll think of something they love to be told, for example. So you have to keep them in state and get them to make a distinction. Ask them if they could have the touch but not the sound, would they feel totally loved? If they had the sound but not the touch, would they feel totally loved? Remember, we need all three. BUT THERE'S ONE THAT OPENS THE VAULT. THERE'S ONE THAT WORKS MAGIC. There's an interesting dynamic that develops in relationships. In the very beginning of a relationship, the stage I call courting, we are very mobilized. We do all three-show, tell, and touch. As time goes on, most people get a little comfortable, and begin to communicate our feelings of love in just the modality we favor-the way we would like to receive it. Problems will arise in a relationship if you're no longer triggering your partner's love strategy-it will feel like some of the magic is missing ...and it is! Most of us think our map of the world is the way it is. We think, "I know what makes me feel loved." That must be what works for everyone else. We forget that the map is not the territory. It's only how we see the territory. Awareness is a very powerful tool. Now that you know how to elicit a love strategy, sit down with your partner and find out what makes him or her feel totally loved, and teach each other how to trigger your love strategies. The changes this understanding can make in the quality of your relationship are worth your investment in this book many times over!

> "*KEY POINTS The key to eliciting strategies is knowing that people will tell you everything you need to know about their strategies. They'll tell you in words. They'll tell you in the way they use their body. They'll even tell you in the way they use their eyes. You can learn to read a person as skillfully as you can learn to read a map or a book. People tend to use a particular part of their neurology visual, auditory, or kinesthetic-more than others. Just as some people are right-handed and others are left-handed, people tend to favor one mode over the others. The key to effective elicitation of a person's strategy is putting the person in a fully "associated" state. State is the hotline to strategy. It's the switch that opens the circuits to a person's unconscious. Love strategies are different from many other strategies in one key way. Instead of a three- or four-step procedure, there's usually only one step. There's one touch, one thing to say, or one way of looking at a person that makes him or her feel totally loved.*"

> "*EXERCISE Once again, much of this chapter is exercises. If you have not elicited your attraction and love strategies, use the tape to do so now. After that, use the page on strategy elicitation to elicit someone else's strategy - buying strategy or motivational strategy, or elicit someone's love strategy. IN OTHER WORDS, APPLY WHAT YOU HAVE LEARNED ABOUT YOURSELF IN THIS CHAPTER TO*

SOMEONE ELSE."

9

PHYSIOLOGY: THE AVENUE OF EXCELLENCE

As we've already seen, one way to get into a resourceful state is through syntax and internal representation. But the biggest leverage we have in any situation is PHYSIOLOGY. Remember, mind and body are totally linked in a cybernetic loop, so the best way to change your state (how you feel) instantly is by changing your PHYSIOLOGY-putting yourself in a powerful physiology. Physiology is the lever to emotional change. In fact, you can't have a change in physiology without a corresponding change in state, and you can't have an emotion without a corresponding change in physiology. We think of states as primarily mental, but in fact, they all have very clear, identifiable physiologies. Think of a depressed person-eyes are generally down (accessing in a kinesthetic mode and/or talking to themselves about all the things that make them depressed), shoulders dropped, and weak, shallow breathing. Depression is a result, and it requires very specific body images to create it. Studies even show that when people get depressed, the biochemical and electrical processes of their bodies are also affected-their immune systems follow suit and become less efficient-their white blood cell count drops. The exciting thing is that you can just as easily create the result called ecstasy by changing your physiology in other specific ways. Smiling and laughing (using the 80 muscles in our face) set off biological processes that make us feel good-they increase the flow of blood to the brain and change the level of oxygen and the level of stimulation of the neurotransmitters. The good news is that you can just pretend, or act "as if" you felt more resourceful, more powerful, and happier than you've ever felt before-"How would I stand, breathe, look, and use my face if I were to act 'as if I felt the best I can feel?"

An important corollary of physiology is congruency. If I'm giving you what I think is a positive message-like "I can handle it"-but my voice is weak and tentative and my shoulders are hunched over and my eyes are down, I'm incongruent, and your unconscious mind will pick up what your conscious mind didn't, and you won't feel confident about my ability. Unconsciously you know that part of me believes I can handle it; and part of me doesn't. I am representing one thing in words and quite another in physiology. But if you say, "I absolutely will do that," and your physiology is unified-that is, your posture, your facial expression, your breathing pattern, the quality of your gestures and movements, and your words and your tonality match-I know you absolutely will do it. One of the best ways to develop congruency is to model the physiologies of people who are congruent-people you respect and admire-watch them in person, or get videotapes of famous people in resourceful states you might want to model. Remember, modeling is about creating possibility. And there's no faster, more dynamic way than through physiology.

"*KEY POINTS The biggest leverage we have in any situation is PHYSIOLOGY. Mind and body are totally linked in a cybernetic loop. Physiology is the lever to emotional change. We think of states as primarily mental, but in fact, they all have very clear, identifiable physiologies. Depression (OR ECSTASY) is a result, and it requires very specific body images to create it. The good news is that you can just pretend, or act "as if,, you felt more resourceful. "How would I stand, breathe, look, and use my face if I were to act 'as if I felt the best I can feel?" An important corollary of physiology is congruency. If I'm incongruent, your unconscious mind will pick up the incongruency even if your conscious mind didn't.*

One of the best ways to develop congruency is to model the physiologies of people who are congruent-people you respect and admire. Remember, modeling is about creating possibility. And there's no faster, more dynamic way than through physiology."

"*EXERCISE Model the physiology of at least two people: 1. A congruent public figure, whom you can get a videotape of. Model the elements of physiology-postures, facial expressions, gestures, voice sounds, words, expressions, phrases 2. An acquaintance or friend who is congruent and has a strong physiology, whom you know well enough to model. Rehearse by yourself, then model some aspects when you are with this person. In both cases, you will begin to notice that you start having feelings that are very similar to the feelings these people have. Choose some elements to adopt in your own physiology, and note your own increase in congruency."*

10

ENERGY: THE FUEL OF EXCELLENCE

You can change your internal representations all day long, but if your biochemistry is messed up, it's going to make the brain create distorted representations. It's going to throw off your whole system. Much of what I will say in this chapter will challenge things you've always believed. I challenge you to apply the SIX PRINCIPLES in this chapter for the next ten to thirty days and judge their validity by the results they produce in your body rather than by what you may have been educated to believe. They are derived from the science of health called Natural Hygiene, and has been around for around 100 years. It is also the foundation of Harvey and Marilyn Diamond's book Flt for Life. FIRST KEY TO LIVING HEALTHTHE POWER OF BREATH The foundation of health is a healthy bloodstream, the system that transports oxygen and nutrients to all the cells of your body. If you have a healthy circulation system, you're going to have a long, healthy life. That environment is the bloodstream. What is the control button for that system? Breathing. It's the way you fully oxygenate the body and thus stimulate the electrical process of each and every cell. If you get nothing else from this chapter but an understanding of the importance of deep breathing, you could dramatically increase the level of your body's health. Dr. Otto Warburg demonstrated that he was able to turn normal, healthy cells into malignant cells simply by lowering the amount of oxygen available to them. Researchers believe that lack of oxygen seems to play a major role in causing cells to become malignant or cancerous. It certainly affects the quality of life of the cells.

Let me share with you the most effective way to breathe in order to cleanse your system. You should breathe in this ratio: inhale one count, hold four counts, exhale two counts. Why exhale for twice as long as you inhale? That's when you eliminate toxins via your lymphatic system. Why hold four times as long? That's how you can fully oxygenate the blood and activate your lymphatic system. The other essential component of healthy overall breathing is daily aerobic exercise ("aerobic" literally means "to exercise with air")-trampolining is one of the best all-weather aerobic exercises. THE SECOND KEY TO LIVING HEALTHTHE PRINCIPLE OF EATING WATER-RICH FOOD Seventy percent of the planet is covered with water. Eighty percent of your body is made up of water. What do you think a large percentage of your diet should contain? You need to make certain that seventy percent of your diet is made up of foods that are rich in water. That means fresh fruits or vegetables, or their juices freshly squeezed. How can you make sure that seventy percent of your diet consists of watercontent foods? It's actually very simple. Just be certain from now on to have a big salad with each meal. Make fruit the snack you reach for instead of a candy bar. THE THIRD KEY TO LIVING HEALTH THE PRINCIPLE OF EFFECTIVE FOOD COMBINING Here's a very simple way to think about it. Eat only one condensed food at a meal. What's a condensed food? It's any food that's not rich in water. Make sure you don't eat starchy carbohydrates and protein at the same meal. Again, you can use Fit for Life as a guide to simple and sensible food combining.

THE FOURTH KEY TO LIVING HEALTH THE LAW OF CONTROLLED CONSUMPTION Want to learn how to eat a lot? Here it is: Eat a little. That way, you'll be around long enough to eat a lot. Dr. Ray Walford (UCLA researcher): "Undernutrition is thus far the only method we know of that consistently retards the aging process and extends the maximum life span of warm-blooded animals." THE FIFTH KEY TO LIVING HEALTH THE PRINCIPLE OF EFFECTIVE FRUIT CONSUMPTION Fruit is the most perfect food. It takes the least amount of energy to digest and gives your body the most in return. The only food your brain can work on is glucose: Fruit is primarily fructose (which can be easily converted into glucose), and it's most often 90-95% water. That means it's cleansing and nurturing at the same time. The only problem with fruit is that most people don't know how to eat it in a way that allows the body effectively to use its nutrients. YOU MUST ALWAYS EAT FRUIT ON AN EMPTY STOMACH. Why? The reason is that fruit is not primarily digested in the stomach. It digests in the small intestine. Fruit is designed to go right through the stomach in a few minutes and into the intestines, where it releases its sugars. But if there is meat or potatoes or starch in the stomach, the fruit gets trapped there and begins to ferment. The best kind of fruit is fresh fruit or freshly squeezed fruit juice. When you wake up, and for as long into the day as is comfortably possible, eat nothing but fresh fruit or freshly squeezed fruit juice. Keep this commitment until at least twelve noon each day. Try it for the next ten days and see for yourself.

THE SIXTH KEY TO LIVING HEALTHTHE PROTEIN MYTH When do you think people are most in need of protein? Probably when they're infants. Mother Nature has provided a food, mother's milk, that supplies the infant with everything it needs. Guess how much of mother's milk is protein-2.38% at birth and reduces to 1.2-1.6% protein in six months! That's all! One of the by-products of protein metabolism is ammonia. Let me mention two points. First, meat contains high levels of uric acid. People with leukemia are usually found to have very high levels of uric acid in their bloodstream. The average piece of meat has 14 grams of uric acid. Your body can only eliminate about 8 grams of uric acid in a day. In addition, do you know what gives meat its taste? Uric acid, from that now dead animal you're consuming. If you doubt this, try eating kosher-style meat before it's spiced. As the blood is drained out, so is most of the uric acid. Meat without uric acid has no flavor. Is that what you want to put in your body, the acid normally eliminated in the urine of an animal? If you absolutely must eat meat, you should get it from a source that guarantees it's pasture grazed, that is, a source that guarantees it doesn't have growth hormones or DES. Second, drastically cut your intake. Make your new maximum one serving of meat per day. Are dairy products any better? In some ways they're even worse. Powerful growth hormones in cow's milk are designed to raise a calf from 90 pounds at birth to a thousand pounds at physical maturity two years later. Researchers say if you want allergies, drink milk. If you want a clogged system, drink milk. The reason, according to Dr. William Ellis, is that few adults can properly metabolize the protein casein in cow's milk. And if you're concerned about calcium, Dr. Ellis suggests eating plenty of green vegetables, sesame butters or nuts-all of which are extremely rich in calcium and easy for the body to use. And remember that it takes four to five quarts of milk to make one pound of cheese. If you must eat cheese, cut up a small amount in a big salad.

One warning: if you start breathing effectively in a way that stimulates your lymph system and you begin to combine your food correctly and eat 70% water-content foods, you may start cleaning out the garbage that's been piling up in your system for years, and it may use its newfound energy to do it as fast as it can. So you might suddenly start sneezing up excess mucus. Does that mean you caught a cold? No, you ate the "cold" you've been creating by years of awful eating habits. Your body may now have the energy to use your eliminative organs to rid itself of excess waste products formerly stored in the tissues and bloodstream. Remember, the quality of our physiology affects our perceptions and behaviors. Take a moment and imagine yourself a month from now having actually followed the principles and concepts we've talked about. See the person you will be after having changed your biochemistry by eating and breathing effectively. What if you felt as if you were living health-and you had energy you never dreamed was possible? If you look at that person and like what you see, then everything I'm offering you is easily within your grasp! It only takes a little discipline-not too much, because once you break your old habits, you'll never go back. For every disciplined effort there's a multiple reward.

***KEY POINTS** You can change your internal representations all day long, but if your biochemistry is messed up, it's going to make the brain create distorted representations. I challenge you to apply the **SIX PRINCIPLES** in this chapter for the next ten to thirty days and judge their validity by the results they produce in your body rather than by what you may have been educated to believe. If you have a healthy circulation system, you're going to have a long, healthy life. That environment is the bloodstream. What is the control button for that system? Breathing. If you get nothing else from this chapter but an understanding of the importance of deep breathing, you could dramatically increase the level of your body's health. You should breathe in this ratio: inhale one count, hold four counts, exhale two counts. You need to make certain that seventy* *percent of your diet is made up of foods that are rich in water. That means fresh fruits or vegetables, or their juices freshly squeezed. How can you make sure that seventy percent of your diet consists of watercontent foods: have a big salad with each meal.Eat only one condensed food at a meal. Want to learn how to eat a lot? Here it is: Eat a little. That way, you'll be around long enough to eat a lot. YOU MUST ALWAYS EAT FRUIT ON AN EMPTY STOMACH. Why? The reason is that fruit is not primarily digested in the stomach. It digests in the small intestine. When you wake up, and for as long into the day as is comfortably possible, eat nothing but fresh fruit or freshly squeezed fruit juice. Keep this commitment until at least twelve noon each day. Try it for the next ten days and see for yourself. Guess how much of mother's milk is protein-2.38% at birth and reduces to 1.2-1.6% protein in six months! Uric acid gives meat its taste. If you doubt this, try eating kosher-style meat before it's spiced. Are dairy products any better? In some ways they're even worse, because of powerful growth hormones in cow's milk.You may start cleaning out the garbage that's been piling up in your system for years. So you might suddenly start sneezing up excess mucus. Does that mean you caught a cold? No, you ate the "cold" you've been creating by years of awful eating habits. See the person you will be after having changed your biochemistry by eating and breathing effectively. What if you felt as if you were living health-and you had energy you never dreamed was possible? Once you break your old habits, you'll never go back. For every disciplined effort there's a multiple reward.*

"EXERCISE Why not commit to the six keys to Living Health for the next ten or thirty days? Ten days is not a long time to apply

these principles, and the health benefits should be incontrovertible even after ten days. Don't you deserve optimum health? Don't you deserve vibrancy in your life? I know you do."

11

LIMITATION DISENGAGE: WHAT DO YOU WANT?

You now know how to direct your mind and support your body. You now know how to achieve whatever you want and how to help others achieve what they want. That leaves a major question. What do you want? What do the people you love and care about want? The second part of this book asks these questions, makes these distinctions, and finds these paths so you can use your abilities in the most elegant, effective, directed ways. You already know how to be an expert marksman. Now you need to find the right target. Powerful tools aren't much use if you don't have a good idea what you want to use them for. When the mind has a defined target, it can focus and direct and refocus and redirect until it reaches its intended goal. I have a question: if you knew you could not fail, what would you do? If you were absolutely certain of success, what activities would you pursue, what actions would you take? There's something rather amazing about what happens when you get a clear internal representation of what you want. It programs your mind and body to achieve that goal. To go beyond our present limitations, we must first experience being more in your minds, and our lives will then follow suit. But before something happens in the external world, it must first happen in the internal world. So if you haven't done the exercise on the tape, do it now. Here's the list so you can see it on paper:

> "1. Start by making an inventory of your dreams, the things you want to have, do, be, and share-play, unlimit! 2. Go over the list you made, estimating when you expect to reach those outcomes-six months, one year, two years, five years, ten years. Twenty years-short term and

long term goals. 3. Pick out the four most important goals for you for this year-pick the things you are most committed to. the most excited about, then write WHY YOU ABSOLUTELY WILL ACHIEVE THEM. 4. Review your four key goals against the five rules for formulating outcomes. (1) State your outcome in positive terms. Say what you want to happen. Too often, people state what they n' want to happen as their goals. (2) Be as specific as possible. How does your outcome look, sound, feel, smell? Engage all of your senses in describing the results you want. The more sensory rich your description, the more you will empower your brain to create your desire. Also be certain to set a specific completion date and/or term. (3) Have an evidence procedure. Know how you will look, how you will feel, and what you will see and hear in your external world after you have achieved your outcome. If you don't know how you'll know when you've achieved your goal, you may already have it. You can be winning and feel like you're losing control if you don't keep score. (4) Be in control. Your outcome must be initiated and maintained by you. It must not be dependent upon other people having to change themselves for you to be happy. Make sure your outcome reflects things that you can affect directly. (5) Verify that your outcome is ecologically sound and desirable. Project into the future the consequences of your actual goal. Your outcome must be one that benefits you and other people.5. Make a list of the important resources you already have at your disposal. 6. Focus in on times you used some of those resources most skillfully. 7. Describe the kind of person you would have to be to attain your goals. 8. In a few paragraphs, write down what prevents you from having the things you desire right now. 9. Take each of your four key goals and create your first draft of a stepby-step plan on how to achieve it. 10. Come up with some models-people who have already done what you want to do. 11. Create your ideal day. 12.Design your perfect environment-sense of place. What would bring out the best of all that you are as a person? Doing these exercises could be the most important steps you can take in your life. You can't reach your outcomes if you don't know what they are. If you get anything from this chapter, it should be this: Results are inevitable. If you don't provide your mind with the programming of the results you desire, someone else will provide that programming for you.You should do one final thing: make a list of the things you already have that were once goals-I call this a gratitude diary. Sometimes people get too fixated on what they want, and they fail to appreciate or use what they already have. The first step toward a goal is seeing what you have, giving thanks for it, and applying it to future achievements."

"KEY POINTS You already know how to be an expert marksman. Now you need to find the right target. Powerful tools aren't much use if you don't have a good idea what you want to use them for. When the mind has a defined target, it can focus and direct and refocus and redirect until it reaches its intended goal. If you knew you could not fail, what would you do? But before something happens in the external world, it must first happen in the internal world. Results are inevitable. If you don't provide your mind with the programming of the results you desire, someone else will provide that programming for you. Make a list of the things you already have that were once goals-I call this a gratitude diary. The first step toward a goal is seeing what you have, giving thanks for it, and applying it to future achievements."

"If you did the goal setting workshop on this tape, you've done quite an exercise. The only piece I could add is a way to create some additional leverage. I call it the "rocking chair" test. Imagine yourself toward the end of your life thinking over your life as you sit in your rocking chair. Would you regret it if you didn't go for any of these four outcomes? Now that you've seen how important these outcomes are to you, how much would you regret not going for them? What things did not happen in your life as a result of not going for these four important things 20, 30, 40, 50 years ago? How will you explain your life to your children or grandchildren? Or did you even have children and grandchildren if you didn't go for any of these outcomes?"

12

POWER OF PRECISION

We've learned that the map is not the territory. The words we use to describe experiences aren't the experiences. They're just the best verbal representation we can come up with. So it stands to reason that one of the measures of success is how accurately and precisely our words can convey what we want-how closely our map can approximate the territory. Just as we all can remember times when words moved us like magic, we can also remember times when our communication went utterly, hopelessly awry. Maybe we thought we were saying one thing, but the other person got the opposite message. So just as precise language has the ability to move people in useful directions, sloppy language can misdirect them. "If thought corrupts language, language can also corrupt thought," wrote George Orwell, whose book 1984 is based on just that principle. Once you know what you want, it helps to be able to know how to get what you want. How do you get whatever you want: ASK! But I don't mean whine or beg or complain or plead or grovel. And I don't mean expect someone else to do your work for you. What I mean is learn to ask intelligently and precisely. Here are five guidelines for asking intelligently and precisely. 1. Ask specifically. How high, how far, how much, when, where, how, with whom? 2. Ask someone who can help you. It's no use trying to borrow a million dollars from someone who makes $50,000/year.

3. Create value for the person you're asking. Figure out how you can help that person first. Don't just ask and expect someone to give you something. 4. Ask with focused, congruent belief. Don't be ambivalent if you aren't convinced about what you're asking for, how can anyone else be? 5. Ask until you get what you want. That doesn't mean asking the same person over and over. Keep changing your approach UNTIL you get what you want.

What's the hardest part of the formula? For many people it's the part about asking specifically. Many phrases and words used by people in our culture have little or no specific meaning. I call these generalized, non-sensory-based words "FLUFF." They're not descriptive language; they're more like vague guesswork. Fluff is "Mary looks depressed," or "Mary is tired." Specific language is "Mary is a thirty-two year old woman with blue eyes and brown hair who is sitting to my right. She's leaning back in her chair, with her eyes defocused and her breathing shallow." It's the difference between giving accurate descriptions of externally verifiable experience and making guesses about what no one else can see. The speaker has no idea what's going on in Mary's mind. He's taking his map and assuming he knows what her experience is. Much of our language is nothing more than wild generalization and assumption. If people tell you with precision what specifically is bothering them, and if you can find out what they want instead, you can deal with it. If they use vague phrases and generalizations, you're just lost in their mental fog. The key to effective communication is to break through that fog, to become a FLUFFBUSTER.

"The closer you are to getting a full representation of the other person's internal experience, the more you can effect change. The best way to deal with verbal fluff is the PRECISION MODEL. Take a few minutes to memorize the diagram. Take your hands one at a time, and move them up and to the left of your eyes so that your eyes are in the position to best visually store this information. Look at your fingers one at a time, and say the words over and over again. Then go to the next finger and the next until you've memorized -one hand. Then do the same for the other. Repeat this process with all your fingers, looking at the phrase and fixing it clearly in your mind."

The precision model is a map of some of the most pernicious wrong turns in communication that people often take. The idea is to notice them and redirect them in a more specific direction. It provides us with the means to qualify people's distortions, deletions, and generalizations WHILE STILL MAINTAINING RAPPORT WITH THEM. Let's start with the pinkies. On the right hand, you have the word "universals." On the left, the words, "all, every, never." Universals are fine-when they're true. If you say that every person needs oxygen, that's different from saying "Kids today have no manners," or "I don't know why I pay these people. They never work." If you hear these universals, you just repeat the statement, emphasizing the universal quantifier: "All kids are ill-mannered?" or "Your employees never work?" the answers will go something like this: "Well, many not all kids-just these particular kids on this block," or "Well, this one guy screwed up, but I guess I can't say that's true for the rest of them." Now bring the next two fingers together and examine the restrictive words "should, shouldn't, must, can't." If someone tells you (s)he can't do something, what signal is (s)he sending to the brain? A limiting one that makes sure, in fact, that (s)he can't do it. If you ask people WHY they can't do something or WHY they have to do something they don't want to do, they usually have no shortage of answers. The way to break the cycle is to say, "What would happen if you were able to do that?" Asking that creates a possibility they were previously unaware of and gets them to consider the positive and negative by-products of the activity. In addition, you could ask, "What prevents me from doing this now?" and thereby become clear about what specifically you need to change. Now go to your middle fingers, which stand for verbs, and if someone says, "I feel depressed," you need to ask them "How, specifically, are you depressed?" or "What, specifically, is causing you to feel that way?"

When you get the person to be more specific, you must often move from one part of the precision model to another. The person may answer your question, "I'm depressed because I always mess up on the job." What's the next question? "You always mess up on your job?" Most likely, the answer will be, "Well, no, not always, I guess." What usually happens is that a person has messed up in some small way and made it symbolize some big failing that exists only in his/her mind. Now put your index fingers together, the ones that represent nouns and "who specifically, what specifically." Whenever you hear nouns-people, places, or things-in any generalized statement like "They don't understand me," ask "Who, specifically" doesn't understand you." If someone says, "Your plan just won't work," you need to find out "what specifically" they have a problem with. A rebuttal like "Yes, it will work" will not maintain rapport or resolve the situation. Often, it's not the whole plan-it's a small part of it. Now press your thumbs together for the last part of the precision model. When we say "too much, too many, too expensive," we're using another form of deletion - a comparison is being made, and we need to find out what the person is comparing. For example, occasionally, someone tells me, "Your seminar is too expensive." When I respond, "Compared to what?" that person might say, "Well, compared to other seminars I've gone to." "How specifically is that seminar like mine?" "Well," he/she replies, "it really isn't." "That's interesting. What would happen if you felt my seminar was really worth the time and money?" His breathing pattern changes, and he/she smiles and says, "I don't know ...I'd feel good, I guess." "What specifically could I do to help you feel that way about my seminar now?" "Well, if you would spend more time on such and such a subject, I probably would feel good about it."

"All right. If I were to spend more time on such and such a subject, would you feel the seminar was worth your time and money?" The person nods in agreement. What's happened in this conversation? We've found the real world, specific points we needed to deal with. We've gone from a string of generalizations to a string of specifics. Here are some additional patterns to listen for. Avoid words like "good," "bad," "better," "worse - words that indicate some form of evaluation or judgment. When you hear phrases like "That's a bad idea" or "It's good to eat everything on your plate," you can respond with "According to whom?" or "How do you know that? Sometimes people will make statements linking cause and effect. They might say, "His comments made me mad," or "The traffic drives me crazy." Now, when you hear those you'll know to ask, "How specifically does X cause Y?" and you will become a better communicator and a better modeler. Another thing to be wary of is verbal mind reading. When someone says, "I just know he loves me," or "I know no one likes me," or "You think I don't believe you," you need to ask, "How do you know that?" The last pattern is a little more subtle-what do words like "attention," "statement," "relationship," "problem" have in common? They are nouns, yes. But we can't find them in the external world. Have you ever seen an "attention" or a "problem" with your eyes? It's not a person, place, or thing. They are processes that have been turned into what we call "nominalizations," and have lost their specificity. When you hear one, you want to turn it back into a process-which gives you the power to redirect and change your experience. If someone says, "I want to change my experience," they way to redirect it is to ask, "What do you want to experience?" If the person responds, "I want love," you would respond with "How (specifically) do you want to be loved?" There are other ways to direct communication by asking the right questions. One is the "OUTCOME FRAME." If you ask someone what's bothering him/her or what's wrong, you'll get a dissertation on just that. If you ask, "What do you want?" or "How do you want to change things?" you've redirected your conversation from the problem to the solution. Here are some "outcome questions":

"What do you want?" "What is the objective?" "What are you here for?" or "What am I here for?" "What do I want for you?" "What do I want me?" Here's another important frame. Choose "how" questions over "why" questions. "Why" questions can get you reasons and explanations and Justifications and excuses. Don't ask your kids why they're having trouble with their algebra. Ask them what they need to do to perform better. The point of this chapter is to show you that there is a specific question or a precise phrase that will transform almost any "problem" in communication if you follow the general principles we've considered here. I always think of the nominalization "problem" as a communication that a person just has an unformulated or unanswered question about something. Find out what specifically they have a question about, and watch the "problem" dissolve.

"KEY POINTS The words we use to describe experiences aren't the experiences. They're ,just the best verbal representation we can come up with. How do you get whatever you want: ASK! I call generalized, non-sensory-based words "FLUFF." They're not descriptive language; they're more like vague guesswork. Fluff is "Mary looks depressed," or "Mary is tired." The closer you are to getting a full representation of the other person's internal experience, the more you can effect change. The Precision Model can also be called the FLUFF-BUSTER! Outcome Frames, Mind Reading, Cause-Effect, Nominalizations are additional distinctions to overcome deletions, distortions, and generalizations."

"EXERCISE Challenge the following examples of "Fluff" (deletions, distortions, and generalizations) with the Precision Model: "People are really inconsiderate."
   "My fear gets in the way."
   "My husband ignores me."
   "My family is driving me crazy."
   "I'm just too serious."
   "I musn't get involved."
   "I never do well on tests."
   "You have to behave appropriately in public."
   or
   "Things have a way of getting messed up."
   "No one treats me with respect."
   "I always show Jane that I love her."
   "I can't understand my wife."
   My son's beliefs worry me."

"What's the use of applying for that job? I just know I don't meet the qualifications."

55

13

THE MAGIC OF RAPPORT

Think of a time when you and another person were completely in sync. Whatever you come up with will be a reflection of the same basic element—rapport. RAPPORT IS THE ABILITY TO ENTER SOMEONE ELSE'S WORLD, to make that person feel that you understand him/her, and that you have a common bond. It's the ability to go fully from your map of the world to his/her map of the world. Rapport is the ultimate tool for producing results with other people. No matter what you want in your life, if you can develop rapport with people, you'll be able to fill their needs, and they will be able to fill yours. All the skills you learn in this book are really ways to achieve greater rapport with people. When people are like each other, they tend to like each other. Whom do most Americans tend to feel better about, the English or the Iranians? In fact, when we say that people are "having differences," we mean that the ways in which they're not alike are causing all sorts of problems. How do we create rapport? We do it by creating or discovering things in common. We call this process "mirroring" or "matching." The most common way to match others is through the exchange of information about each other through words. However, studies have shown that only 7% of what is communicated between people is transmitted through the words themselves. 38% comes through the tone of voice. 55% of communication, the largest part, is the result of physiology or body language. The facial expressions, the gestures, the quality and type of movements of the person delivering a communication provides us with much more about what they're saying than the words do by themselves. What if you use all three linked together? While the words are working on a person's conscious mind, the tonality and physiology are working on the unconscious. That's where the brain is thinking, "Hey, this person's like me.

(S)he must be okay." And because it's unconscious, it's even more effective. You're not aware of anything but the bond that's been formed.

So, how do you mirror another person's physiology? What kinds of physical traits can you mirror? Start with the voice. Mirror the tonality and phrasing, the pitch, how fast (s)he talks, what sort of pauses the person makes, the volume. Mirror favorite words or phrases. How about posture and breathing patterns, or eye contact, body language, facial expressions, hand gestures, or other distinctive movements? Any aspect of physiology, from the way a person plants their feet to the way (s)he tilts their head, is something you can mirror. What if you could mirror everything about another person? Do you know what happens? People feel as though they've found their soul mate, someone who totally understands, who can read their deepest thoughts, who is just like them. But you don't have to mirror everything about a person to create a state of rapport. If you just start with the tone of voice or a similar facial expression, you can learn to build incredible rapport with anyone. When you break it down, there are two keys to mirroring-keen observation and personal flexibility. Representational systems provide keys to a secret code. There are verbal cues, like the ones on the next page, for example:

"*Of course, breathing and posture patterns, speed and selectivity of speech, will accompany these verbal patterns. The person who is talking about "how this looks" to them (visual) will probably be breathing high in the chest, speaking rapidly with shallow breathing, might be pointing, and may have hunched shoulders and an extended neck, while auditory people will more resonant voices and their breathing will tend to be more even and deep, coming from the diaphragm or the whole chest, and will have balanced muscle tension, and may fold their arms, and tilt their heads slightly to one side. Kinesthestic people speak in a slow tempo, will take long pauses between words so they can get a feel for what they're saying in their low, deep tonalities. Much of their body movement will tend to indicate tactile or external kinesthetic accessing. They often have upturned palms with arms bent and relaxed with a solid posture with their heads sitting squarely on their shoulders. In case you're concerned about mirroring another person, you're not giving up your identity. Mirroring simply creates a commonality of physiology that underscores our shared humanity. When I'm mirroring, I can get the benefits of another person's feelings and experiences and thoughts. That's a powerful, beautiful, and empowering lesson to experience about how to share the world with other human beings. Studies of successful people have shown over and over again that they have a great talent for creating rapport. Those who are flexible and attractive in all three modalities can affect large numbers of people whether as a teacher, a businessperson, or a world leader. By practicing consistently, you enter the world of whomever you're with and speak in that person's mode. It will soon become second nature. And you will do it without any conscious thought. In fact, because of what's known as PACING AND LEADING, you will be able to get them to follow you. Once you have mirrored someone for a while (paced them), you can change your physiology and behavior almost instinctively as the other person changes, and you create a link that can almost be felt. Leading comes just as naturally as pacing (mirroring). You reach a point where you start to initiate change rather than just mirroring the other person, a point where you have developed so much rapport that when you change, the other person will unconsciously follow you. Sometimes, by mirroring someone's anger, for example, you can enter that person's world so strongly that when you begin to relax, that person will relax as well. Remember, rapport doesn't just mean you're smiling. Rapport means responsiveness. Occasionally you may need to be just as intense in your communication to a person, since the challenge to you is one of the many ways respect is developed in his/her part of the culture."*

Flexibility is the key to establishing rapport. Remember, the biggest barrier to rapport is thinking that other people have the same map you do, that because you see the world one way, they do, too. Excellent communicators rarely make this mistake. If you fail to communicate to someone, it's tempting to assume that that person is a hopeless fool who refuses to listen to reason. But that virtually guarantees you'll never get through. One essential tenet of what we teach is that THE MEANING OF YOUR COMMUNICATION IS THE RESPONSE YOU ELICIT. The responsibility in communication rests upon you. There's a final wonderful thing about the magic of rapport. It's the most accessible skill in the world. You don't need textbooks, and you don't need courses. The only tools you need are you eyes, your ears, your senses of touch, smell, and taste. We are always communicating and interacting. Rapport is simply doing both in the most effective ways possible. You can use rapport at the grocery store. You can use it at your job and at home. If, when you go in for a job interview, you match and mirror the interviewer, (s)he'll like you immediately. If you want to become a master communicator, all you need to do is learn how to enter other people's worlds. You already have everything you need to do it now.

KEY POINTS

"RAPPORT IS THE ABILITY TO ENTER SOMEONE ELSE'S WORLD. All the skills you learn in this book are really ways to achieve greater rapport with people (including yourself). When people are like each other, they tend to like each other. Studies have shown that only 7% of what is communicated between people is transmitted through the words themselves. 38% comes through the tone of voice. 55% of communication, the largest part, is the result of physiology or body language. What if you could mirror everything about another person? People feel as though they've found their soul mate. There are two keys to mirroring-keen observation and personal flexibility. Representational systems provide keys to a secret code of matching and mirroring. Mirroring creates a commonality of physiology that underscores our shared humanity. When I'm mirroring, I can get the benefits of another person's feelings and experiences and thoughts.Because of what's known as PACING AND LEADING, once you have established rapport (pacing), you will be able to get them to follow your lead when you make a change in your physiology. Remember, rapport doesn't just mean you're smiling. Rapport means responsiveness. The biggest barrier to rapport is thinking that other people have the same map you do, that because you see the world one way, they do, too. THE MEANING OF YOUR COMMUNICATION IS THE RESPONSE YOU ELICIT. The responsibility in communication rests upon you. Rapport is the most accessible skill in the world. You don't need textbooks, and you don't need courses. The only tools you need are you eyes, your ears, your senses of touch, smell, and taste. We are always communicating and interacting. Rapport is simply doing both in the most effective ways possible-all you need to do is learn how to enter other people's worlds."

EXERCISE

"*Unfortunately, the only way to practice rapport skills is just to go out and DO IT! Commit yourself to matching and mirroring people-begin with friends, stretch yourself, and amaze yourself at what you can do without them being aware of what you're doing. Then start getting bolder, try a business associate-unless you're bold from the start. Practice before it's a matter of life and death. You don't want to try your rapport skills for the first time with a terrorist hijacker! Just remember, there's never an excuse to be bored in a business meeting again! There are always people to match and mirror, to pace and to lead.*"

14
DISTINCTIONS OF EXCELLENCE: METAPROGRAMS

"In the right key one can say anything. In the wrong key, nothing: the only delicate part is the establishment of the key." -George Bernard Shaw Why do people react so differently to identical messages? Why does one person see the glass as half-empty and another see it as half-full? Shaw s quote is precisely right. If you address someone in the right key, you can do anything. If you address someone in the wrong key, you can do nothing. If you want to be a master communicator or a master persuader, you have to know how to find the right key. The path is through metaprograms. Metaprograms are powerful internal patterns that help determine how people form internal representations and direct their behavior. Metaprograms are the internal programs (or sorts) we use in deciding what to pay attention to. We distort, delete, and generalize information because the conscious mind can only pay attention to so many pieces of information at any given time. To communicate effectively with a person, you have to understand his/her metaprograms. The FIRST METAPROGRAM involves MOVING TOWARD something or MOVING AWAY. All human behavior revolves around the urge to gain pleasure or avoid pain. One person may walk a mile to work because (s)he enjoys the exercise. Another may walk because of a terrible phobia about being in a car.

As with the other metaprograms I'll discuss, this process is not one of absolutes. Everyone moves toward some things and away from others. Some people tend to be energetic, curious risk takers. They may feel most comfortable moving toward something that excites them. Others tend to be cautious, wary, and protective; they see the world as a more perilous place. To find out which way people move, ask them, "WHAT DO YOU WANT IN A RELATIONSHIP -A HOUSE, CAR, JOB, OR ANYTHING ELSE?" Do they tell you what they want or what they don't want. What does this information mean? Everything. If you're a business person selling a product, you can promote it two ways, by what it does or by what it doesn't do. Use the wrong metaprogram with a person, and you might as well have stayed at home. Let's say you want your child to spend more time on his/her schoolwork. You might say, "You better study or you won't get into a good college." How well will the strategy work? It depends on your child. If (s)he is primarily motivated by moving away, it might work well. But what if your child moves toward things? Try saying, "If you do this, you can pick and choose any college you want to." The SECOND METAPROGRAM deals with EXTERNAL and INTERNAL FRAMES OF REFERENCE. Ask people how they know they've done a good job. For some people, the proof comes from the outside. The boss pats you on the back and says your work was great, for example. When you get that sort of external approval, you know your work is good. That's an EXTERNAL FRAME OF REFERENCE. For others, the proof comes from the inside. They "just know inside" when they've done well. For example, you might do a job that gets a lukewarm reception from your boss or peers, but if you feel it's good work, you'll trust your own instincts rather than theirs. That's an INTERNAL FRAME OF REFERENCE. It's important to note that all these metaprograms are CONTEXT- and STRESS-RELATED. If you've done something for ten years, you probably have developed a strong internal frame of reference; if you're brand new, you may not have as strong an internal frame of reference about what is right or wrong in that context.

The THIRD METAPROGRAM involves SORTING BY SELF or SORTING BY OTHERS. Some people look at human interactions primarily in terms of what's in it for them personally, some in terms of what they can do for themselves and others. Of course, people don't always fall into one extreme or other. If you sort only by self, you become a self-absorbed egotist. If you sort only by others, you become a martyr. In a service business, you obviously need people who sort by others. If you're hiring an auditor, you might want someone who would sort by self. It's like a doctor who sorts strongly by self. He may be a brilliant diagnostician, but unless you feel (s)he cares about you, (s)he won't be totally effective. In fact, someone like that would probably be better off as a researcher than as a clinician. Putting the right person in the right job remains one of the biggest problems in American business. But it's a problem that could be dealt with if people knew how to evaluate the ways that job applicants processed information. The key is to observe people as carefully as possible, listen to what they say, what sort of metaphors they use, what their physiology reveals, when they're attentive and when they're bored. People reveal their metaprograms on a consistent, ongoing basis. To determine if people sort by self or others, see how much attention they pay to other people. Do they lean toward people and have facial expressions that reflect concern for what others are saying, or do they lean back and remain bored and unresponsive? The FOURTH SORTING PROGRAM involves MATCHERS and MISMATCHERS. Look at these figures and tell me how they relate to each other.

If I asked you to describe the relationship between the three figures, you could answer in many ways. You could say they're all rectangles and they all have four sides. If you see them that way, I would call you a MATCHER. Some people respond to the world by finding SAMENESS. They look at things and see what they have in common-MATCHERS. Another kind of matcher will find SAMENESS WITH EXCEPTION-"they're all rectangles, but one is lying down and the other two are standing up." Other people are MISMATCHERS-DIFFERENCE people. There are two kinds of them. One type looks at the world and sees how things are different. That person might look at the figures and say they are all different and have different relationships to each other. They're not alike at all. The other kind of mis-matcher sees DIFFERENCE WITH EXCEPTION. That kind of MISMATCHER is like the MATCHER who finds SAMENESS WITH EXCEPTION IN REVERSE-(s)he sees the differences first, and then add the things they have in common. So who's right? They both are, of course: it all depends on a person's perception. However, mis-matchers often have difficulty creating rapport with people because they are always creating differences. Remember, rapport is about finding things in common. The next metaprogram involves what it takes to CONVINCE SOMEONE OF SOMETHING. The convincer strategy has two parts. You must first find out what sensory building blocks a person needs to become convinced, and then you must discover how often a person has to receive these stimuli before becoming convinced. To discover someone's CONVINCER METAPROGRAM, ask "How do you know when someone else is good at a job? Do you have to a) see them or watch them do it, b) hear about how good they are, c) do it with them, or d) read about their ability?" The answer may be a combination of these.

The next question is "How often does someone have to demonstrate he/she is good before you're convinced?" There are four possible answers: a) immediately (for example, if they demonstrate that they're good at something once, you believe them, b) a number of times (two or more), c) over a period of time (say, a few weeks or a month or a year), and d) consistently. In the last case, a person has to demonstrate that (s)he is good each and every time. Another metaprogram is POSSIBILITY versus NECESSITY. Some people are motivated primarily by necessity, rather than by what they want. They do something because they must. They're not pulled to take action by what is possible. Others are motivated to look for possibilities. They're motivated less by what they have to do than by what they want to do. They seek options, experiences, choices, paths. The person who is motivated by necessity is interested in what's known and what's secure. The person who is motivated by possibility is equally interested in what's not known. WORK-STYLE METAPROGRAM. Some people are not happy unless they're INDEPENDENT. They have great difficulty working closely with other people and can't work well under a great deal of supervision. They have to run their own show. Others function best as part of a group. We call their strategy a COOPERATIVE one. They want to share responsibility for any task they take on. Still others have a PROXIMITY strategy, which is somewhere in between. They prefer to work with other people while maintaining sole responsibility for a task. They're in charge but not alone. One of the keys to success in anything is the ability to make new distinctions. Metaprograms give you the tools to make crucial distinctions in deciding how to deal with people, and you're not limited to the metaprograms I've listed here. For example, some people sort primarily by feelings and others sort by logical thoughts. Would you try to persuade them the same way?

Some people make decisions based only on specific facts and figures. First they have to know if the parts will work-they'll think about the broader picture later. Others are convinced first by an overall concept or idea. They react to global chunks. They want to see the big picture first. If they like it, then they'll think about the details. Some people are turned on by beginnings. They're most excited when they get a new idea off the ground, and then they soon tend to lose interest in it and go on to something else. Others are fixated on completion. Anything they do they have to see all the way to the end. A person who sorts primarily by people will talk mostly about the people at the wedding or the people in a film. A person who sorts primarily by activities will talk about what actually happened at the wedding, what happened in the film, and so on. The other thing an understanding of metaprograms provides is a model for balance. We all follow one strategy or another for using metaprograms. What a metaprogram does is tell your brain what to delete. To change your metaprograms, all you have to do is become aware of the things you normally delete. And begin to focus your attention on them. In other words, you can change a metaprogram by consciously deciding to do so. You might want to stretch a little. You can start thinking about things that appeal to you and actively move toward them, for example, if you tend to move away. The other way to change a metaprogram is by Significant Emotional Events-"SEES." If you sorted by necessity and missed out on some great job opportunity because the company was looking to someone with a dynamic sense of possibility, you might be shocked into changing your approach. Like everything else in this book, metaprograms should be used on two levels. The first is as a tool to calibrate and guide our communication with others. Just as people's physiology will tell you countless stories about them, their metaprograms will speak eloquently about what motivates them and what frightens them off'. The second is a tool for personal change. Remember, you are not your behaviors. If you tend to run any kind of pattern that works against you, all you have to do is change it. Metaprograms offer one of the most useful tools for personal calibration and change.

KEY POINTS

"*Metaprograms are the internal programs (or sorts) we use in deciding what to pay attention to and what we delete. All human behavior revolves around the urge to gain pleasure or avoid pain. In sales, use the wrong metaprogram with a person, and you might as well have stayed at home. All these metaprograms are CONTEXT- and STRESS-RELATED. People reveal their metaprograms on a consistent, ongoing basis. For example, to determine if people sort by self or others, do they lean toward people or do they lean back and remain unresponsive? Some people respond to the world by finding SAMENESS, others find DIFFERENCE. So who's right? It all depends on a person's perception. The person who is motivated by necessity is interested in what's known and what's secure. The person who is motivated by possibility is equally interested in what's not known.To change your metaprograms, all you have to do is become aware of the things you normally delete. And begin to focus your attention on them-in other words, you can change a metaprogram by consciously deciding to do so. Just as people's physiology will tell you countless stories about them, their metaprograms will speak eloquently about what motivates them and what frightens them off. Remember, you are not your behaviors. If you tend to run any kind of pattern that works against you, all you have to do is change it."*

Nuevo
EXERCISE

"Elicit someone's metaprograms in two areas of their lives: professional and personal. Here are the questions that go with each of the metaprograms in this chapter: 1. DIRECTION METAPROGRAM: TOWARD or AWAY Question: "What do you want in a ________ (job or relationship, etc.)?" Note whether the person tells you what they WANT or what they DON'T WANT. 2. EXTERNAL/INTERNAL METAPROGRAM Question: "How do you know you've done a good job?" (This same question can apply for either a professional or personal context) Note whether they respond based on their own INTERNAL feelings about themselves or whether they listen primarily to the EXTERNAL world. 3. SELF VERSUS OTHERS METAPROGRAM There is no question for this metaprogram. You discover this metaprogram by observing whether someone pays attention to others in terms of their use of physiology-leaning in towards someone or back from someone-and their apparent concern for others as opposed to concern for themselves.

4. MATCHING VERSUS MISMATCHING METAPROGRAM Question: "What is the relationship between these three figures?" (see page 117 for the three figures). You can also ask the question, "What is the relationship between your life now and a year ago?" Note whether they focus on the sameness or the differences, and whether they respond with both-sameness with exception, or difference with exception. 5. CONVINCER METAPROGRAM Question #1: "How do you know someone else is good at a job?" Question #2: "How often does someone have to demonstrate he/she is good at something before you're convinced?" Note V or A or K for question # 1, TIME distinctions on question #2-see above in the summary. 6. POSSIBILITY VERSUS NECESSITY METAPROGRAM Question: "Why did you choose your present job?" Note whether they do something because they want to (the POSSIBILITIES) or because they have to or should (NECESSITY).

7. WORK STYLE METAPROGRAM Question: "Would you tell me about a-work situation in which you were the happiest?" Note whether they liked working INDEPENDENTLY, with others but have sole responsibility for their tasks (PROXIMITY), or a COOPERATIVE desire to share responsibility for everything."

15
HOW TO HANDLE RESISTANCE AND SOLVE PROBLEMS

This chapter is about handling resistance and solving problems. If there was a key word in the first half of the book, it was "modeling." If there's a key word for a second half of this book, it's "flexibility"-the one thing effective communicators have in common. Flexibility doesn't necessarily come naturally. Most of us think of settling a dispute as something akin to verbal boxing. Much more elegant is not to overcome force, but to align yourself with the force directed at you and guide it in a new direction-the metaphor of the Oriental martial arts like aikido and t'ai chi. Remember that there is no such thing as resistance, there are once inflexible communicators. It's important for us to remember that certain words and phrases create resistance and problems. Let me give you the example of one ever-present, three-letter word- "but." If someone says, "That's true, but...", or worse, "I love you ...but..." what is that person saying? The word "but" has negated everything said before it. What if you simply substitute the word "and" instead? What if you say, "That's true, and here's something else that's also true"? Instead of creating resistance, you've created an avenue of redirection. What would happen if you had a communication tool you could use to communicate exactly how you felt about an issue, without compromising your integrity in any way, and yet you never had to disagree with the person either? Well, here it is: it's called the AGREEMENT FRAME. It consists of three phrases you can use in any communication to respect the person you're communicating with, maintain rapport with that person, share with him/her what you feel is true, and yet never resist that person's opinion in any way.This chapter is about handling resistance and solving problems. If there was a key word in the first half of the book, it was "modeling." If there's a key word for a second half of this book, it's "flexibility"-the one thing effective communicators have in common. Flexibility doesn't necessarily come naturally. Most of us think of settling a dispute as something akin to verbal boxing. Much more elegant is not to overcome force, but to align yourself with the force directed at you and guide it in a new direction-the metaphor of the Oriental martial arts like aikido and t'ai chi. Remember that there is no such thing as resistance, there are once inflexible communicators. It's important for us to remember that certain words and phrases create resistance and problems. Let me give you the example of one ever-present, three-letter word- "but." If someone says, "That's true, but...", or worse, "I love you ...but..." what is that person saying? The word "but" has negated everything said before it. What if you simply substitute the word "and" instead? What if you say, "That's true, and here's something else that's also true"? Instead of creating resistance, you've created an avenue of redirection. What would happen if you had a communication tool you could use to communicate exactly how you felt about an issue, without compromising your integrity in any way, and yet you never had to disagree with the person either? Well, here it is: it's called the AGREEMENT FRAME. It consists of three phrases you can use in any communication to respect the person you're communicating with, maintain rapport with that person, share with him/her what you feel is true, and yet never resist that person's opinion in any way.

Here are the three phrases: "I APPRECIATE AND..." "I RESPECT AND..." "I AGREE AND..." In each case you're doing three things. You're building rapport by entering the other person's world and acknowledging his/her communication rather than ignoring or denigrating it with words like "but" or "however." You're creating a frame of agreement that bonds you together. And you're opening the door to redirecting something without creating resistance. For example, someone says to you, "You're absolutely wrong." Instead of losing rapport by saying, "No, I'm not wrong," respond this way: "I respect the intensity of your feelings about this, and I think if you were to hear my side of it you might feel differently." Notice, you don't have to agree with the content of the person's communication, but you can always appreciate, respect, or agree with someone's feeling about something. You can appreciate that person's feeling because if you were in the same physiology, if you had the same perception, you would feel the same way. You can also appreciate someone else's intent. For example, many times two people on opposite sides of an issue don't appreciate each other's points of view, so they don't even hear each other. But if you use the agreement frame, you will find yourself listening more intently to what the other person is saying-and discovering new ways to appreciate people as a result. One way to solve problems-is to redefine them-to find a way to agree rather than to disagree. Another way is to BREAK THEIR PATTERNS. I've found that confusion is one of the greatest ways to interrupt patterns. For example, there was a pattern interrupt in an antismoking campaign of a few years ago. It suggested that anytime someone you love reaches for a cigarette, give him/her a kiss instead.Here are the three phrases: "I APPRECIATE AND..." "I RESPECT AND..." "I AGREE AND..." In each case you're doing three things. You're building rapport by entering the other person's world and acknowledging his/her communication rather than ignoring or denigrating it with words like "but" or "however." You're creating a frame of agreement that bonds you together. And you're opening the door to redirecting something without creating resistance. For example, someone says to you, "You're absolutely wrong." Instead of losing rapport by saying, "No, I'm not wrong," respond this way: "I respect the intensity of your feelings about this, and I think if you were to hear my side of it you might feel differently." Notice, you don't have to agree with the content of the person's communication, but you can always appreciate, respect, or agree with someone's feeling about something. You can appreciate that person's feeling because if you were in the same physiology, if you had the same perception, you would feel the same way. You can also appreciate someone else's intent. For example, many times two people on opposite sides of an issue don't appreciate each other's points of view, so they don't even hear each other. But if you use the agreement frame, you will find yourself listening more intently to what the other person is saying-and discovering new ways to appreciate people as a result. One way to solve problems-is to redefine them-to find a way to agree rather than to disagree. Another way is to BREAK THEIR PATTERNS. I've found that confusion is one of the greatest ways to interrupt patterns. For example, there was a pattern interrupt in an antismoking campaign of a few years ago. It suggested that anytime someone you love reaches for a cigarette, give him/her a kiss instead.

"There are two main ideas in this chapter. The first is that you can persuade better through agreement than through conquest. The competition model is very limited. I've already talked about the magic of rapport and how essential it is to personal power. If you see someone as a competitor, someone to be vanquished, you're starting out with the exact opposite framework. Everything I know about communication tells me to build from agreement, not from conflict; to learn to align and lead rather than to try and overcome resistance. The second idea is that our behavior patterns aren't indelibly carved into our brain. If we repeatedly do something that limits us, we're just running a terrible pattern over and over again. The solution is simply to interrupt the pattern. In both cases, the common ground is the idea of flexibility.

Elegance in an argument is not to overcome force, but to align yourself with the force directed at you and guide it in a new direction. There is no such thing as resistance, there are only inflexible communicators. It's important for us to remember that certain words and phrases create resistance and problems. Let me give you the example of one ever-present, three-letter word-"but." How does, "I love you ...but..." make you feel? Instead of creating resistance, you've created an avenue of redirection by replacing "but" with "and." The AGREEMENT FRAME allows you to communicate exactly how you feel about an issue, without compromising your integrity in any way, and makes it so you never have to disagree with anyone either. "I APPRECIATE AND..." "I RESPECT AND..." "I AGREE AND..."

"I respect the intensity of your feelings about this, and I think if you were to hear my side of it you might feel differently." Notice, you don't have to agree with the content of the person's communication. You can always appreciate, respect, or agree with someone's feeling about something. You can also appreciate someone else's intent. If you use the agreement frame, you will find yourself listening more intently to what the other person is saying-and discovering new ways to appreciate people as a result. One way to solve problems is to redefine them-to find a way to agree rather than to disagree. Another way is to break their patterns. Confusion is one of the greatest ways to interrupt patterns. Everything I know about communication tells me to build from agreement, not from conflict; to learn to align and lead rather than to try and overcome resistance."

Our behavior patterns aren't indelibly carved into our brain. If we repeatedly do something that limits us, we're just running a terrible pattern over and over again. The solution is simply to interrupt the pattern.

EXERCISE

"1. Use the AGREEMENT FRAME for at least one full day, and note both the responses in others, and what happens to your own resistance levels as a result i.e. how hard is it to feel like you're arguing? 2. Come up with creative ways to break people's patterns. With friends and family, you can be outrageous, with others you might want to create confusion. If someone is really depressed, I tend to ask them things as outrageous as "Is that a bugger in your nose?"

16

REFRAMING: THE POWER OF PERSPECTIVE

If I asked you, "What does a footstep mean?" you would probably answer, "It doesn't mean anything to me." But what if you're sitting home alone late at night, and you hear footsteps downstairs? A moment later, you hear the steps moving toward you. Do the footsteps have meaning then? They sure do. The same signal (the sound of footsteps) will have many different meanings depending upon what it has meant to you in similar situations in the past. Thus the meaning of any experience in life depends upon the frame we put around it. If you change the frame we put around it the context, the meaning changes instantly. One of the most effective tools for personal change is learning how to put the best frames on any experiences. This process is called reframing.If I asked you, "What does a footstep mean?" you would probably answer, "It doesn't mean anything to me." But what if you're sitting home alone late at night, and you hear footsteps downstairs? A moment later, you hear the steps moving toward you. Do the footsteps have meaning then? They sure do. The same signal (the sound of footsteps) will have many different meanings depending upon what it has meant to you in similar situations in the past. Thus the meaning of any experience in life depends upon the frame we put around it. If you change the frame we put around it the context, the meaning changes instantly. One of the most effective tools for personal change is learning how to put the best frames on any experiences. This process is called reframing.

Reframing in its simplest form is changing a negative statement into a positive one by changing the frame of reference used to perceive the experience. There are two major types of reframes, or ways to alter our perception about something: context reframing and content reframing. Context reframing involves taking an experience that seems to be bad, upsetting, or undesirable and showing how the same behavior or experience is actually a great advantage in another contextFor example, oil was once considered something that destroyed the value of land for crop usage. Yet look at its value today. Content reframing involves taking the exact same situation and changing what it means. For example, you might say your son never stops talking. He never shuts up! After content reframing, you might say that he certainly must be a very intelligent young man to have so much to say. Another kind of content reframe is to actually change the way you see, hear, or represent a situation. If you're upset about what someone said to you, you may envision yourself smiling as he says the same negative words expressed in the tonality of your favorite singer. Unlimited Power is full of reframes. "The Seven Lies of Success" is a whole chapter of reframes. Think of a major mistake you've made in the last year. You might feel an instant rush of gloom. But chances are the mistake was part of an experience with more successes than failures. And, as you consider it, you'll begin to realize you probably learned more from that mistake than from anything else you did that month. So you can zero in on what you did wrong, or you can reframe the experience in a way that focuses beyond it to what you have learned. There are multiple meanings to any experience. One of the keys to success is finding the most useful frame for any experience so you can turn it into something that works for you rather than against you.Reframing in its simplest form is changing a negative statement into a positive one by changing the frame of reference used to perceive the experience. There are two major types of reframes, or ways to alter our perception about something: context reframing and content reframing. Context reframing involves taking an experience that seems to be bad, upsetting, or undesirable and showing how the same behavior or experience is actually a great advantage in another contextFor example, oil was once considered something that destroyed the value of land for crop usage. Yet look at its value today. Content reframing involves taking the exact same situation and changing what it means. For example, you might say your son never stops talking. He never shuts up! After content reframing, you might say that he certainly must be a very intelligent young man to have so much to say. Another kind of content reframe is to actually change the way you see, hear, or represent a situation. If you're upset about what someone said to you, you may envision yourself smiling as he says the same negative words expressed in the tonality of your favorite singer. Unlimited Power is full of reframes. "The Seven Lies of Success" is a whole chapter of reframes. Think of a major mistake you've made in the last year. You might feel an instant rush of gloom. But chances are the mistake was part of an experience with more successes than failures. And, as you consider it, you'll begin to realize you probably learned more from that mistake than from anything else you did that month. So you can zero in on what you did wrong, or you can reframe the experience in a way that focuses beyond it to what you have learned. There are multiple meanings to any experience. One of the keys to success is finding the most useful frame for any experience so you can turn it into something that works for you rather than against you.

Take a moment to reframe these situations: 1. My boss yells at me all the time. 2. I had to pay $4,000 more in income tax this year than last year. 3. We have little or no extra money to buy Christmas presents this year. 4. Every time I begin to succeed in a big way, I sabotage my success. Here are some possible reframes. 1a. It's great he cares enough to tell you how he feels. He could have just fired you. 2a. That's great. You must have made a lot more money this year than last year. 3a. Great! Then you can become much more ingenious and make something people will never forget instead of buying run-of-the-mill gifts. Your gifts will be personal. 4a. It's great that you're so aware of what your pattern has been in the past. Now you can figure out what triggered it and change it forever! Most reframing is done for us, not by us. Someone else changes the frame for us and we react to it. What is advertising, after all, but a huge industry with the sole purpose of framing and reframing mass perceptions? Do you really think there is anything particularly macho about a specific brand of beer or particularly sexy about a particular cigarette?Take a moment to reframe these situations: 1. My boss yells at me all the time. 2. I had to pay $4,000 more in income tax this year than last year. 3. We have little or no extra money to buy Christmas presents this year. 4. Every time I begin to succeed in a big way, I sabotage my success. Here are some possible reframes. 1a. It's great he cares enough to tell you how he feels. He could have just fired you. 2a. That's great. You must have made a lot more money this year than last year. 3a. Great! Then you can become much more ingenious and make something people will never forget instead of buying run-of-the-mill gifts. Your gifts will be personal. 4a. It's great that you're so aware of what your pattern has been in the past. Now you can figure out what triggered it and change it forever! Most reframing is done for us, not by us. Someone else changes the frame for us and we react to it. What is advertising, after all, but a huge industry with the sole purpose of framing and reframing mass perceptions? Do you really think there is anything particularly macho about a specific brand of beer or particularly sexy about a particular cigarette?

Few of us spend much time thinking about how to frame our communications with ourselves. Something happens to us. We form an internal representation of the experience. And we figure that's what we have to live with. Think how crazy that is. It's like turning on the ignition, starting up your car, and then seeing where it decides to go. You need to start framing and reframing experiences in a way that makes them work for you. Reframing can be used to eliminate negative feeling about nearly anything. A phobia, for example, is often rooted at a deep kinesthetic level, so you need to provide more distance from it in order to do an effective reframe. The way to deal with people who are phobic is to disassociate them from their representations several times. We call this double disassociation. For example, if you have a phobia about something, do the exercise on the tape that will take you step by step through a process that can free you of fears and phobias in a matter of minutes.Few of us spend much time thinking about how to frame our communications with ourselves. Something happens to us. We form an internal representation of the experience. And we figure that's what we have to live with. Think how crazy that is. It's like turning on the ignition, starting up your car, and then seeing where it decides to go. You need to start framing and reframing experiences in a way that makes them work for you. Reframing can be used to eliminate negative feeling about nearly anything. A phobia, for example, is often rooted at a deep kinesthetic level, so you need to provide more distance from it in order to do an effective reframe. The way to deal with people who are phobic is to disassociate them from their representations several times. We call this double disassociation. For example, if you have a phobia about something, do the exercise on the tape that will take you step by step through a process that can free you of fears and phobias in a matter of minutes.

SIX STEP REFRAME

"1. Identify the pattern or behavior you wish to change. 2. Establish communication with the part of your unconscious mind that *generates the behavior. Ask yourself the question, "Will the part of me that generates behavior X be willing to communicate with me in consciousness and give me a signal in body sensations, visual images, or sounds." Now test the response by asking the part to communicate yes ...and then no ...so that you can distinguish between the two responses. 3. Separate intention from behavior. Thank the part for its willingness to cooperate with you. Now ask it if it would be willing to let you know what it's been trying to do for you be generating behavior X. 4. Create alternative behaviors to satisfy intention. Go inside and contact the most creative part of you and ask it to generate three alternative behaviors that are just as good or better than behavior X for satisfying the intention of the part we've been communicating with. Now ask the creative part if it would be willing to reveal to you what the three new behaviors are. 5. Have part X accept the new choices and the responsibility for generating them when needed.*

6. Make an ecological check. Go inside and ask if there are any parts that object to the negotiations that have just taken place or if all parts agree to support you. Then step into the future and imagine a situation that would have triggered the old behavior, and experience using one of your new choices and still achieving the benefits you desire. If you get a signal that other parts object to these new choices, you must start at the beginning, identify which part is objecting, what benefits it's been giving you in the past, and have it work with part X to generate new choices that would maintain the benefits it's always given you and also provide for you a new set of choices."

Almost any seemingly negative experience can be reframed into a positive one. How often have you said, "Someday I'll probably look back and laugh at this." Why not look back and laugh at it now? It's all a matter of perspective. It's important to note that you can reprogram someone's representation through swish patterns and other techniques, but if the person gets greater benefits from the old behavior than from the new choices, the person will probably return to the old behavior. I don't want you to only think of reframing as a therapy, as a way of going from situations you consider bad to ones you consider good. Reframing is really nothing more or less than a metaphor for potential and possibility. There are very few things in your life that can't be reframed into something better. One of the most important frames to consider is possibilities. Make a list of five things you're doing right now that you're pretty pleased with. Then imagine them as even better. Possibility reframing is something we can all do. We all know people who are reverse reframers. No matter how bright the silver lining, they can always find a dark cloud. But for every disabling attitude, for every counterproductive behavior, there's an effective reframe. You don't like something? Change it.

KEY POINTS

"*Thus the meaning of any experience in life depends upon the frame we put around it. If you change the frame we put around it the context, the meaning changes instantly. One of the most effective tools for personal change is learning how to put the best frames on any experiences. This process is called REFRAMING. Reframing in its simplest form is changing a negative statement into a positive one by changing the frame of reference used to perceive the experience. There are two major types of reframes, or ways to alter our perception about something: context reframing and content reframing. Unlimited Power is full of reframes. "The Seven Lies of Success" is a whole chapter of reframes. There are multiple meanings to any experience. One of the keys to success is finding the most useful frame for any experience so you can turn it into something that works for you rather than against you. What is advertising, after all, but a huge industry with the sole purpose of framing and reframing mass perceptions? Do you really think there is anything particularly macho about a specific brand of beer or particularly sexy about a particular cigarette?*"

"*The way to deal with people who are phobic is to disassociate them from their representations several times. One important thing to remember about refraining is that all human behaviors have a purpose in some context. In some cases you may find it impossible to reframe the behavior without confronting the underlying need that the behavior fulfills. I want to make sure that I create for them new behavioral choices that will fill their needs without negative side effects, How often have you said, "Someday I'll probably look back and laugh at this." Why not look back and laugh at it now? It's all a matter of perspective. If the person gets greater benefits from the old behavior*" *than from the new choices, the person will probably return to the old behavior. Reframing is really nothing more or less than a metaphor for potential and possibility. There are very few things in your life that can't be refrained into something better.* **"**

We all know people who are reverse reframers. No matter how bright the silver lining, they can always find a dark cloud. But for every disabling attitude, for every counterproductive behavior, there's an effective reframe. You don't like something? Change it.

EXERCISE

1. DO A SIX STEP REFRAME! This is a powerful tool and will help you establish RAPPORT with your subconscious mind. 2. Think about five things in your life that bother you, and REFRAME them in your mind-things like the "My boss yells at me all the time" example in this chapter.

17

ANCHORING YOURSELF TO SUCCESS

A flag, like countless other things in our environment, is an anchor, a sensory stimulus linked to a specific set of states. An anchor can be a word or a phrase or a touch or an object. It can be something we see, hear, taste, or smell. Anchors have great power because they can instantly access powerful states. Our world is full of anchors, some of them profound, some of them trivial. If I start to say to you, "Winston tastes good like a..." chances are you'll automatically say, "Cigarette should." Anchoring is a way to give an experience permanence. We can change our internal representations or our physiology in a moment and create new results, but those changes require conscious thought. However, with anchoring you can create a consistent triggering mechanism that will automatically cause you to create the state you desire in any situation without your having to think about it. Anchoring is the most effective technique I know for constructively channeling our powerful unconscious reactions so they're always at our disposal. We all anchor regularly. In fact, it's impossible not to. All anchoring is a created association of thoughts, ideas, feelings, or states with a specific stimulus. Remember Pavlov's dogs? We live in a stimulus/response world, where much of human behavior consists of unconscious programmed responses. So how do anchors get created? Whenever a person is in an intense state where the mind and body are strongly involved together and a specific stimulus is consistently and simultaneously provided at the peak of the state, the stimulus and the state become neurologically linked. Then, anytime the stimulus is provided, the intense state automatically results. Not all anchors are positive association by any means. How do you feel when you see a red flashing light in your rear view mirror? Does it instantly and automatically change your state?

One of the things that affects the power of an anchor is the intensity of the original state. Sometimes people have such an intense unpleasant experience-like fighting with their spouse or boss-that from then on, whenever they see that person's face, they immediately feel anger inside-and from that point on their relationship or job loses all its joy. There are two simple steps to consciously create a positive anchor for yourself or others. First you must put yourself, or the person you're anchoring, into the specific state you wish to anchor. Then you must consistently provide a specific, unique stimulus as the person experiences the peak of that state. Another way to create a positive anchor-let's say a confidence anchor-is to ask that person to remember a time when (s)he felt the state (s)he wishes to have available on cue, then have that person step back into that experience so that (s)he is fully associated and can feel those feelings in the body. As the person does this, you will begin to see changes in physiology-facial expressions, posture, breathing. As you see these states nearing their peak, quickly provide a specific and unique stimulus several times. KEYS TO ANCHORING: 1. INTENSITY OF THE STATE 2. TIMING (PEAK OF EXPERIENCE) 3. UNIQUENESS OF STIMULUS 4. REPLICATION OF STIMULUS

1. FOR AN ANCHOR TO BE EFFECTIVE, WHEN YOU PROVIDE THE STIMULUS, YOU MUST HAVE THE PERSON IN A FULLY ASSOCIATED, CONGRUENT STATE, WITH HIS/HER WHOLE BODY FULLY INVOLVED. I call this an intense state The more intense, the easier it is to anchor, and the longer the anchor will last. 2. YOU MUST PROVIDE THE STIMULUS AT THE PEAK OF THE EXPERIENCE. If you provide an anchor too soon or too late, you won't capture the full intensity. 3. YOU SHOULD CHOOSE A UNIQUE STIMULUS. It's essential that the anchor gives a clear and unmistakable signal to the brain-a handshake, for example, would not be very unique. 4. FOR AN ANCHOR TO WORK, YOU MUST REPLICATE IT EXACTLY.

ANCHORING EXERCISE

Stand up and think of a time when you were totally confident, when you knew you could do whatever you wanted to do. Put your body in the same physiology it was in then. Stand the way you did when you were totally confident. At the peak of that feeling, make a fist and say, "Yes!" with a strength and certainty. Breathe the way you did when you were totally confident. Again make the same fist and say, "Yes!" in the same tonality. Now speak in the tone of a person with total confidence and control. As you do this, create the same fist and then say, "Yes!" in the same way. If you can't remember a time, think of how you would be if you did have such an experience. Put your body in the physiology it would be in if you did know how to feel totally confident and in control. Breathe the way you would if you felt total confidence.

Now as you stand there in a state of total confidence, at the height of that experience, gently make a fist and say, "Yes!" in a powerful tone of voice. Be aware of the power at your disposal, of the remarkable physical and mental resources you have, and feel the full surge of that power and centeredness. Start over and do this again and again, five or six times, each time feeling stronger, creating an association in your neurology between this state and the act of making a fist and saying, "Yes!" Then change your state, change your physiology. Now make your fist and say, "Yes!" in the same way as you did when you anchored, and notice how you feel. Do that several times over the next few days. Get yourself into the most confident, powerful state you're aware of, and at the peak of those states make a fist in a unique way. You should also have resourceful states available at your fingertips. Select three to five states that you would like to have available, then anchor them to a specific part of yourself so that you have easy access to them. Let me give you a few techniques for handling negative anchors. One is to fire off opposing anchors at the same time. We call this COLLAPSING ANCHORS. Anchor a series of resourceful states in one part of your body, then anchor the unresourceful state on a different part of your body, then trigger both anchors at the same time. You'll find something remarkable happens. The brain connects the two in your nervous system; then, finny time either anchor is touched, it has the choice of two responses. And the brain will almost always choose the more positive response. Either it will put you in the positive state, or you'll go into a neutral state (in which both anchors have canceled each other out). Now, if you've just been reading this workbook, or just listening to the tapes WITHOUT DOING THESE ANCHORING EXERCISES, they'll seem silly. But if you do them, you'll be able to see the incredible power they have. This is a key ingredient of success: THE ABILITY TO ELIMINATE FROM YOUR OWN ENVIRONMENT TRIGGERS THAT TEND TO PUT YOU IN NEGATIVE OR UNRESOURCEFUL STATES, WHILE INSTALLING POSITIVE ONES IN YOURSELF AND IN

OTHERS.

One of the ways to do this is to make a chart of the major anchors-positive and negative-in your life. Note whether they're primarily triggered by visual, auditory, or kinesthetic stimuli. Once you know what your anchors are, you should go about collapsing the negative ones and making best use of the positive ones. Think of the power you could have in your own life if you could take the things that used to bother you and have them make you feel great or resourceful enough to change them. You have the power to do it.

KEY POINTS

Anchors have great power because they can instantly access powerful states. Our world is full of anchors. "Winston tastes good like a..." How do you feel when you see a red flashing light in your rear view mirror? Does it instantly and automatically change your state? Anchoring is a way to give an experience permanence. With anchoring you can create the state you desire in any situation without your having to think about it. All anchoring is a created association of thoughts, ideas, feelings, or states with a specific stimulus. Remember Pavlov's dogs? Whenever a person is in an intense state where the mind and body are strongly involved together and a specific stimulus is consistently and simultaneously provided at the peak of the state, the stimulus and the state become neurologically linked. Then, any time the stimulus is provided, the intense state automatically results.

KEYS TO ANCHORING: 1. INTENSITY OF THE STATE 2. TIMING (PEAK OF EXPERIENCE) 3. UNIQUENESS OF STIMULUS 4. REPLICATION OF STIMULUS This is a key ingredient of success: THE ABILITY TO ELATE FROM YOUR OWN ENVIRONMENT TRIGGERS THAT TEND TO PUT YOU IN NEGATIVE OR UNRESOURCEFUL STATES, WHILE INSTALLING POSITIVE ONES IN YOURSELF AND IN OTHERS.

EXERCISE

"There are many ANCHORING exercises on the tape, including: 1. Select three to five states or feelings that you would like to have at your fingertips, then ANCHOR them to a specific part of yourself so that you have easy access to them. Remember the importance of INTENSITY,

TIMING, UNIQUENESS, and the ability to REPLICATE the anchor exactly. 2. Continue STACKING ANCHORS on your fist. 3. Anchor three different people in positive states-have them remember a time when they were (exuberant, confident, loving, ecstatic, centered, proud, grateful, etc.). and anchor them several times in the same state. Then engage them in a conversation and test the anchor while they are distracted. If they return to the state you've anchored, CONGRATULATIONS. If they don't, check the FOUR KEYS TO ANCHORING-especially the INTENSITY OF THE STATE, and anchor again. 4. COLLAPSE UNRESOURCEFUL ANCHORS. Listen to the part of the tape when I have you put the resource states in one hand, and the unresourceful state in the other hand."

18

VALUE HIERARCHIES: THE ULTIMATE JUDGMENT OF SUCCESS

In order to truly change, grow, and prosper, we need to become consciously aware of the rules we have for ourselves and others, of how we really measure or judge success or failure. This is the power of the final and critical element called VALUES. What are values? Simply, they are your own private, personal, and individual beliefs about what feelings are most important to you. Your values are your belief systems about right, wrong, good and bad. Our values are the feelings we all fundamentally need to move toward. That feeling of congruity, or personal wholeness and unity, comes from the sense that we are fulfilling our values by our present behavior. They even determine what you will move away from. They determine how you will respond to any given experience in life. Values are like the executive level of judgment in the human brain-they are the master key to unleashing the magic within. Most of your values have been programmed through punishment/reward, but the challenge for most people is that many of these values are unconscious. People feel very uncomfortable and suspicious of individuals who have values very different from their own. All of us have a bottom line-things that are more important to us above anything else. For some people it's honesty; for others it's friendship. Some people may lie to protect a friend, even though honesty is important to them. How can they do this? Because friendship is higher on their ladder of importance (hierarchy of values) than honesty in this context. You may place a high personal value onbusiness success, but also on having a close family life. So conflict occurs when you promise to be with your family one evening and then a business opportunity arises. What you choose to do depends on what you place as your highest value at the time. So rather than saying it is bad to spend time on business and not on your family or vice versa, just discover what your values truly are. There's no real success except in keeping with your basic values. Sometimes it's a matter of learning how to mediate between existing values that are in conflict. To deal effectively with people, we need to know what's most important to them, specifically what their hierarchy of values is. Most people are totally unaware of the values of their loved ones. You can't fill someone else's needs if you don't know what they are. How do you discover your own or someone else's values? First. you need to place a frame around the values you are looking for. That is, you need to elicit them in a specific context. We often have different values for work, relationships, or family. You must ask, "WHAT'S MOST IMPORTANT TO YOU ABOUT A PERSONAL RELATIONSHIP?" The person might answer, "The feelings of support." Then you might ask, "What's important about support?" S/he might respond, "It shows that someone loves me." You might ask, "What's important about someone loving you?" S/he might answer, "It creates feelings of joy for me." Then, to have a clear understanding of someone's hierarchy of values, all you need to do is take this list of words ("support". "love", "joy") and compare them. Ask, "Which is more important to you? Being supported or feeling joy?" If the answer is, "Feeling joy," then obviously it is higher in the hierarchy of values. Next you would ask, "Which is more important to you, feeling joy or being loved?" etc . I've listed some values that are important to me in relationships as a guide for you to practice with. (You don't have to use this list you may have additional ones, or totally different ones). Rank these values in order of importance.

LOVE ECSTASY MUTUAL COMMUNICATION RESPECT FUN GROWTH SUPPORT CHALLENGE CREATIVITYBEAUTY ATTRACTION SPIRITUAL UNITYFREEDOM HONESTY For example, which is more important to you, love or ecstasy? If the answer is love, is it more important than mutual communication? You need to go completely through the list and see if anything is more important than the value you begin with. If not, it's at the top of the hierarchy. Then, go on to the next word on the list. What means more to you, ecstasy or mutual communication? If the answer is ecstasy, continue down the list, comparing it with the next word. As you see, ranking is not always an easy process. If the distinctions are not clear, ask what would happen if you took away one value. "If you could never be ecstatic but you could grow, would that be your choice, or if you could never grow but you could be ecstatic, which one would you want more?" Putting together one of your own value hierarchies is one of the most valuable exercises in this book. When you have finished, check how you feel about the list you've created. Is it accurate in your estimation? You can elicit other people's values in casual conversation. One simple but invaluable technique is to listen carefully to the words people use. People tend to use over and over key words that denote values at the top of their hierarchy-like "creativity" or "joy" or "freedom," etc.

It's crucial for managers to know the highest values of their employees. To elicit them, the first thing to ask is, "What would it take to cause you to join an organization?" Let's say the employee answers, "A creative environment." "What else would it take?" Then you would want to know, even if all of those existed, what would cause him/her to leave. Suppose the answer is, "A lack of trust." If you asked, "even if there were a lack of trust, what would make you stay," and (s)he answered, "Nothing, I'd be out of there," then you know that person highest value. Also, it's critical to note a person's evidence procedure or rule in order to determine how your concept of trust differs from their. (S)he may believe there is only trust if they're never questioned in their decisions. Remember, when we use words, we're using a map-and the map is not the territory. Your map, your complex equivalence, your rule may be very different from my rules about what has to happen to have a value like "freedom," for example. Freedom for me may mean being able to do whatever I want, whenever I want, wherever I want, with whomever I want, as much as I want. Freedom for you may mean having someone take care of you all the time, being free from hassles by living in a structured environment. Freedom for someone else might be a political construct, the discipline needed to maintain a particular political system. So it's absolutely critical that you construct a map that's as accurate as possible-you need to discover the rules for what has to happen in order to get the value. So you ask the question, " WHAT HAS TO HAPPEN FOR YOU TO GET (VALUE)?" The more specific you are in your rules or evidence procedures the better. Let's say the value is "romance," and your rule is that to have romance, you have to have a good relationship with an attractive and loving woman. But maybe you have a more specific picture (unconsciously, perhaps): a tempestuous romance with a blond, blue-eyed Playboy bunny with a 42 inch bust, a Fifth Avenue condo in Manhattan, and a six-figure income. Would it be valuable to know your rule? You bet. And your chances for getting your value of romance may be slim with that evidence procedure or rule. There's an important thread about values and rules: flexibility. Remember, in any context, the system with the most flexibility, with the most choices, will be the most effective. It is relatively easy to change your evidence procedure. When you were a high school kid, maybe freedom meant trying to imitate Warren Beatty's sex life. But perhaps now a loving relationship provides the comfort, the resources, and the joy that embody more real freedom than the ability to jump into bed with any person you meet at a bar. Often, incongruity comes not from the value themselves, but from the evidence procedures or rules. Success and spirituality don't have to produce incongruity. You can be a great success and still have a rich spiritual life. But what if your rule for success is having a big mansion, and your rule for spirituality is living a simple, austere life? You'll have to either redefine your evidence procedures or rules, or reframe your perception. Otherwise, you could be dooming yourself to a life of inner conflicts. Discovering someone's values is simply a matter of finding out what is most important to him or her. In knowing that, you can more effectively know not just their needs but your own.

KEY POINTS

"That feeling of congruity, or personal wholeness and unity, comes from the sense that we are fulfilling our values by our present behavior. VALUES determine how you will respond to any given experience in life. Values are like the executive level of judgment in the human brain. Most of your values have been programmed through punishment/ reward, but the challenge for most people is that many of these values are unconscious. All of us have a bottom line-things that are more important to us above anything else. What you choose to do depends on what you place as your highest value at the time. In order to elicit someone's values, just keep asking, "WHAT'S MOST IMPORTANT TO YOU ABOUT (specific context-like relationships, job, etc.)?" Then, to have a clear understanding of someone's hierarchy of values, all you need to do is take this list of words ("support", "love", "joy") and compare them. Ask, "Which is more important to you? or ?Remember, when we use words, we're using a map-and the map is not the territory. Your

map, your complex equivalence, your rule, may be very different from my rules about what has to happen to have a value like "freedom," for example. Often, incongruity comes not from the value themselves, but from the evidence procedures or rules. Success and spirituality don't have to produce incongruity. But what if your rule for success is having a big mansion, and your rule for spirituality is living a simple, austere life? You'll have to either redefine your evidence procedures or rules, or reframe your perception. Otherwise, you could be dooming yourself to a life of inner conflicts."

EXERCISE

"*1. Discover your LIFE VALUES by asking yourself the question, "WHAT'S MOST IMPORTANT TO ME IN LIFE?" 2. Then discover the HIERARCHY OF YOUR LIFE'S VALUES, by comparing your list ("WHAT'S MOST IMPORTANT IN MY LIFE- OR ?") 3. Once you have a HIERARCHY OF YOUR LIFE'S VALUES, discover the EVIDENCE PROCEDURES or RULES by asking the question, "WHAT HAS TO HAPPEN FOR ME TO HAVE (the VALUE)?*

"

19

THE FIVE KEYS TO WEALTH AND HAPPINESS

You now have the resources to take absolute charge of your life. You have the ability to form the internal representations and produce the states that lead to success and power. There are certain experiences that time and time again put people in unresourceful states. There are experiences that consistently prevent people from being all they can be. I want to give you a map showing where the perils are and what you need to know to overcome them. I call these the FIVE KEYS TO WEALTH AND HAPPINESS. There's nothing profound about them, but they're absolutely crucial. THE FIRST KEY TO WEALTH AND HAPPINESSMUST LEARN HOW TO HANDLE FRUSTRATION Frustration can kill dreams. You must learn to discipline your frustration. Let me tell you something. The key to success is massive frustration. Look at almost any great success, and you'll find there's been massive frustration along the waylook at Federal Express. All successful people learn that success is buried on the other side of frustration. You have the tools to handle frustration in an effective way. ,Take the images that once frustrated you and make them wither and disappear and change them to the images that bring you ecstasy, or reframe the meaning of the things that used to frustrate you-what can you learn from them, what new opportunities for growth do they provide? etc.

THE SECOND KEY TO WEALTH AND HAPPINESSYOU MUST LEARN HOW TO HANDLE REJECTION The biggest challenge for people in our culture is that they can't handle the word "no." Remember the question I asked earlier? What would you do if you knew you could not fail? Remember, you have the tools to anchor yourself so the word "no" turns you on. You can take any rejection and turn it into an opportunity. THE THIRD KEY TO WEALTH AND HAPPINESSYOU MUST LEARN TO HANDLE FINANCIAL PRESSURE The only way not to have financial pressure is not to have any finances. You should be able to deal with money as with anything else in your mind, with the same purpose and elegance. Learn to earn, to save, and to give. THE FOURTH KEY TO WEALTH AND HAPPINESSYOU MUST LEARN HOW TO HANDLE COMPLACENCY Comfort can be one of the most disastrous emotions a body could have. What happens when people get too comfortable? They stop growing. stop working, stop creating value. Ray Kroc said, "When you're green you grow; when you ripen, you rot." Some complacency comes from comparison. LEARN TO JUDGE YOURSELF BY YOUR GOALS INSTEAD OF BY WHAT YOUR PEERS SEEM TO BE DOING.

"Speak with good purpose only," and "don't major in minor things"-don't waste your time gossiping and speculating about what's wrong with other people. Doing that is a great strategy for becoming complacent about your own goals. THE FIFTH KEY TO WEALTH AND HAPPINESS ALWAYS GIVE MORE THAN YOU EXPECT TO RECEIVE This may be the most important key of all because it virtually guarantees true happiness. The key to any relationship, for example. is that you have to give first and then keep giving. Don't stop and wait to receive. The biggest illusion about success is that it's like a pinnacle to be climbed, a thing to be possessed, or a static result to be achieved. If you want to succeed, you have to think of success as a process, a way of life, a habit of mind, a strategy for life.

-KEY POINTS

"*There are experiences that consistently prevent people from being all they can be. I want to give you a map showing where the perils are and what you need to know to overcome them. I call these the FIVE KEYS TO WEALTH AND HAPPINESS. # 1: HOW TO HANDLE FRUSTRATION #2: HOW TO HANDLE REJECTION #3: YOU MUST LEARN TO HANDLE FINANCIAL PRESSURE #4: HOW TO HANDLE COMPLACENCY #5: ALWAYS GIVE MORE THAN YOU EXPECT TO RECEIVE 2. THINGS I FEAR REJECTION ABOUT: Solution tool: 3. WAYS IN WHICH I EXPERIENCE FINANCIAL PRESSURE Solution tool: 4. WHERE IN MY LIFE DO I HAVE COMPLACENCY? Solution tool:*

5. WHERE IN MY LIFE IS THERE AN OPPORTUNITY TO GIVE that would improve the quality of life for me and the people I care about? Solution tool: Ask yourself "What, specifically, could I give that I am not currently giving that I could afford-either financially or emotionally-to give that would EMPOWER that relationship?"

20

TREND CREATION: THE POWER OF PERSUASION

"We are not going to be able to operate our SPACESHIP EARTH successfully nor for much longer unless we see it as a whole spaceship and our fate as common. It has to be everybody or nobody." -Buckminster Fuller In a world full of persuaders, you can be one, too, or you can be someone who gets persuaded. You can direct your life or be directed. This book has really been about persuasion. Power today is the ability to communicate and the ability to persuade. If you're a persuader with no legs, you'll persuade someone to carry you. If you have no money, you'll persuade someone to lend you some. Persuasion may be the ultimate skill for creating change. In the modern world, persuasion isn't a choice. It's an ever-present fact of life. The difference in our children's behavior may be the difference between who is a greater persuader-you and I or the drug pusher. If you abdicate responsibility, there are plenty of others ready to do the persuading. One day when I started thinking about all of the "problems" of the world, I got very excited because I noticed a common relationship to them all-they're all behavioral problems! I hope you're using your precision model right now and are asking, "All?" If the source of the problem is not human behavior, there is usually a behavioral solution. For example, crime is not the problem-it's people's behavior that creates this thing we call crime. The way human beings behave is what creates or prevents war. Famine is not the problem in Africa. Human behavior is the problem. Destroying each other's land does not support the creation of a larger food supply.

We also know that the states from which behavior springs are the result of their internal representations. We are now living in an age where the technology to communicate messages to almost the entire world is already in place and being used. The technology is the media-radio, television, movies, and print. Therefore, the means to change massive numbers of people's internal representations, and thus massive numbers of people's states, and thus massive numbers of people's behaviors, is available to us now. What if the same power and technology that could get massive numbers of individuals to fight could be used effectively to bridge value differences and represent the unity of all peoples? Don't get me wrong-I'm not suggesting that this is easy. What I am suggesting is that the mechanisms for change are as available as the tools for destruction. I am suggesting that we become more conscious of what we see, hear, and experience on a consistent basis and that we pay attention to how we represent these experiences to ourselves individually and collectively. What we consistently represent on a mass scale tends to become internalized in mass numbers of people. Thus, if we want to create a world that works, we might want to consistently review and plan what we can do to create representations that empower us on a unified global scale. We have more power now than ever before to shape the inner perceptions that govern behavior. Trend creation is what leadership is all about, and it's the real message of this book. If you really want to make a difference, you need to know how to be a leader, how to take these persuasion skills and make the world a better place. That means being a more positive, more skillful model for your kids, for your employees, for your business associates, for your world. This book is definitely about maximizing your personal power, learning how to be effective and successful in what you try to do. But there's no value to being a sovereign of a dying planet. Ultimate power is synergistic. It comes from people working together, not working apart to create a better world for our global community.

KEY POINTS

"*In a world full of persuaders, you can be one, too, or you can be someone who gets persuaded. In the modern world, persuasion isn't a choice. It's an ever-present fact of life. The difference in our children's behavior may be the difference between who is a greater persuader-you and I or the drug pusher. I got very excited because I noticed a common relationship to all of the "problems" of the world-they're all behavioral problems! We know that the states from which behavior springs are the result of internal representations. We are now living in an age where the technology to communicate messages to almost the entire world is already in place and being used. The technology is the media-radio, television, movies, and print. Therefore, the means to change massive numbers of people's internal representations, and thus massive numbers of people's states, and thus massive numbers of people's behaviors, is available to us now. What we consistently represent on a mass scale tends to become internalized in mass numbers of people. There's no value to being a sovereign of a dying planet. Ultimate power is synergistic. It comes from people working together, not working apart to create a better world for our global community."*

EXERCISE

"Write a paragraph in response to the following questions: 1. "How can I be a better leader in my life RIGHT NOW?" The answer can be very simple-better role model for your kids by doing something specific. Or it can be major-leading in the community in the area of ecology by recycling. Or you could decide to be a world leader in a certain area if that's a step you can really take now. Make it real for you-things you have the ability to do RIGHT NOW. 2. Step five years into the future. "What could you see yourself doing in terms of TREND CREATION and LEADERSHIP five years from now?" Be SPECIFIC and make it a five year goal if you come up with some things that you are PASSIONATE about."

21

LIVING EXCELLENCE: THE HUB CHALLENGE

Let's review what you've learned in this book. You know now that the most powerful tool on the planet is the biocomputer between your two ears. Properly run, your brain can make your life greater than any dream you've ever had before. You've learned the Ultimate Success Formula: Know your outcome, take action, develop the sensory acuity to know what you're getting, and change your behavior until you get what you want. You've learned that we live in an age where fabulous success is available to all of us, but that those who achieve it are those who take action. Knowledge is important, but it's not enough. Plenty of people had the. same information as a Steve Jobs or a Ted Turner. But the ones who took action created fabulous success and changed the world. You've learned about the importance of modeling. You can learn by experience, by trial and error-or you can speed up the process immeasurably by learning how to model. Every result produced by an individual was created by some specific set of actions in some specific syntax. You can greatly decrease the time it takes to master something by modeling the internal actions (mental) and external actions (physical) of people who produce outstanding results. In a few hours or a few days or few years, depending on the type of task, you can learn what took them months or years to discover. You've learned that the quality of your life is the quality of your communication. Communication takes two forms. The first is your communication with yourself. The meaning of any event is the meaning you give it. You can send your brain powerful, positive, empowering signals that will make everything work for you, or you can send your brain signals about what you can't do. People of excellence can take any situation and make it work for them-people like W. Mitchell, Julio Iglesias, Captain Gerald Coffee, who can take terrible tragedy and turn it into triumph. We can't go back in time. We can't change what actually happened. But we can control our representations so they'll give us something positive for the future. The second form of communication is with others. The people who've changed our world have been master communicators. You can use everything in this book to discover what people want so you can become an effective, masterful, elegant communicator. You've learned about the awesome power of belief. Positive beliefs can make you a master. Negative beliefs can make you a loser. And you've learned that you can change your beliefs to make them work for you. You've learned about the power of state and the power of physiology. You've learned the syntax and strategies that people use, and you've learned how to establish rapport with anyone you meet. You've learned powerful techniques for reframing and anchoring. You've learned how to communicate with precision and skill, how to avoid the fluff language that kills communication, and how to use the precision model to get others to communicate effectively with you. You've learned about handling the five roadblocks in the way of success. And you've learned about the metaprograms and values that serve as the organizing principles for personal behavior. Life has a processional effect. Changes lead to more changes. Like a rock thrown into the still pond, you create ripples that grow larger in the future. Think of two arrows pointing in the same general direction. If you make a tiny change in the direction of one of them, if you push it three or four degrees in a different direction, the change may be imperceptible at first. But if you follow that path for yards and then miles, there will barely seem to be a relationship between the first path and the second path. If you use even one of the principles in this book today, you've taken a step. You've set a cause in motion, and every cause creates an effect or result, and every result piles on the last one to take us in a direction. Every direction carries with it an ultimate destination. Here's a final question to consider. In what direction are you presently heading? If you follow your current direction, where will you be in five years or ten years? And is that where you want to go? If this book has taught you anything, it's the possibility of creating positive change with almost lightning speed-on both a personal and a global level.

Unlimited power doesn't mean you always succeed or that you never fail. Unlimited power just means you learn from every human experience and make every experience work for you in some way. It is unlimited power to change your perceptions, to change your actions, and to change the results you're creating. I'd like to suggest another way to change your life and ensure continued success. Find a team you want to play on. Ultimate power is the power of people working together, not pulling apart. That might mean your family, or it might mean good Friends. It could be trusted business partners or people you work with and care about. If you ask people about their richest experiences in life, they'll usually come up with something they did as part of a team. Being on a team makes you stretch. it makes you grow. If you're alive, you're already on some team. It can be your family, your relationship, your business, your city, your country, your world. You can sit on the bench and watch, or you can get up and play. My advice to you is be a player. Join the hunt. Share your world. Because the more you give, the more you get. And make sure you're on the team that challenges you. It's easy for things to get off track. If you can surround yourself with people who will never let you settle for less than you can be, you have the greatest gift that anyone can hope for. Association is a powerful tool. Make sure the people you surround yourself with make you a better person by your association with them. Once you have a commitment to a team, the challenge of excellence is to become a leader. My last challenge for you is to share this information with others. There are two reasons. First, we all teach what we most need to learn. By sharing an idea with others, we get to hear it again and remind ourselves of what we value and believe is important in life. The other reason is there is incredible, almost unexplainable, richness and joy that comes from helping another person make a truly important and positive change in his/her life. So that's the ultimate message of this book. Be a doer. Take charge. Take action. Use what you've learned here, and use it now. Don't just do it for you-do it for others as well. There were two great orators of antiquity. One was Cicero, the other Demosthenes. When Cicero was done speaking, people always gave him a standing ovation and cheered, "What a great speech!" When Demosthenes was done, people said, "Let us march," and they did. That's the difference between presentation and persuasion. I hope to be classified in the latter category.

If you listen to these tapes and read this workbook and think, "Wow, that was great: they're a lot of great tools," and don't use anything you've heard or read, we've wasted our time together. However, if you start right now and go back through this workbook that summarizes the tapes and provides you with dozens of exercises to change your perception and your behavior, and use it as a handbook to changing anything you want to change, then you may have begun a life journey that will make even the greatest dreams of your past seem almost trivial. I challenge you to make your life a masterpiece. I challenge you to join the ranks of those people who live what they teach, who walk their talk. They are models of excellence the rest of the world marvels about. Someday maybe I'll get to tell your story, and if these tapes and workbook help you move in that direction, I'll consider myself very lucky indeed.

KEY POINTS

"*Life has a processional effect. Changes lead to more changes. Like a rock thrown into the still pond, you create ripples that grow larger in the future. Think of two arrows pointing in the same general direction. If you make a tiny change in the direction of one of them . . . If you use even one of the principles in this book today, you've taken a step. You've set a cause in motion, and every cause creates an effect or result, and every result piles on the last one to take us in a direction. Every direction carries with it an ultimate destination. In what direction are you presently heading? If you follow your current direction, where will you be in five years or ten years? And is that where you want to go? If this book has taught you anything, it's the possibility of creating positive change with almost lightning speed-on both a personal and a global level. Find a team you want to play on.*

Being on a team makes you stretch, it makes you grow. If you're alive, you're already on some team. It can be your family, your relationship, your business, your city, your country, your world. You can sit on the bench and watch, or you can get up and play. My advice to you is be a player. Because the more you give, the more you get. And make sure you're on the team that challenges you. If you can surround yourself with people who will never let you settle for less than you can be, you have the greatest gift that anyone can hope for. Association is a powerful tool. Make sure the people you surround yourself with make you a better person by your association with them. Once you have a commitment to a team, the challenge of excellence is to become a leader. _ We all teach what we most need to learn. By sharing an idea with others, we get to hear it again and remind ourselves of what we value and believe is important in life.

There is incredible, almost unexplainable, richness and joy that comes from helping another person make a truly important and positive change in his/her life. "What a great speech!" versus "Let us march." That's the difference between presentation and persuasion. I challenge you to make your life a masterpiece."

"1. Write a paragraph in response to the following questions (if you didn't answer them when I asked you on the tape): "In what direction are you presently going? If you follow your current direction, where will you be in five years? In ten years? Is that where you want to go? If not, what do you need to change? 2. Make a list of people that are on your team. How could you let them know they're on your team? What little things (or big things) could you do for them to let them know? Does your current team challenge you? If not, look for some people to ADD TO YOUR TEAM that will challenge you to be the most you can be. Make sure the people that are on your team REALLY KNOW you count them as part of your team!"

Meanwhile, I leave you with a simple Irish blessing: May the road rise to meet you. May the wind be always at your back. May the sun shine warm on your face, the rains fall soft upon your fields, and, until we meet again, may God hold you softly in the palm of His hand.